FREDERICK AND POTSDAM

A City is Born

FREDERICK AND POTSDAM

A City is Born

Commissioned by the state capital of Potsdam
Potsdam Museum – Forum für Kunst und Geschichte
Edited by Jutta Götzmann

POTSDAM MUSEUM   FORUM FÜR KUNST UND GESCHICHTE

HIRMER PUBLISHERS

Contents

This catalogue is published to accompany the exhibition "Friedrich und Potsdam – Die Erfindung (s)einer Stadt" [Frederick and Potsdam – a City is Born] from August 20 until December 2, 2012 in the Potsdam Museum – Forum für Kunst und Geschichte, Am Alten Markt 9, 14467 Potsdam

Foreword

To mark the tercentenary of Frederick's birth and to inaugurate its new location on the Alter Markt, the Potsdam Museum – Forum für Kunst und Geschichte is staging the special exhibition "Friedrich und Potsdam – die Erfindung (s)einer Stadt" [Frederick and Potsdam – a City is Born]. The intention is to demonstrate, in this historic place, the significance of Frederick II for the destiny of Potsdam, the garrison city which he made a royal residence, and its city-planning, architectural and social development. The exhibition concentrates on the king as the man who commissioned buildings for Potsdam, who promoted manufacturing in the city, in particular the production of courtly luxury and utilitarian goods, and on the lasting consequences of these policies for the city and its inhabitants.

The Old City Hall is itself one of the most important exhibits. The exhibition on 500 sq. m. of the ground floor is structured into five thematic sections. Here it can be seen how Frederick the Great improved not only the Alter Markt as a public square, but also expanded the city by magnificent building projects including more than 600 houses for the citizenry. The exhibition opens with a contemporary view of the city during Frederick's reign, which lasted from 1740 to 1786. In the process we learn about their opinions on the city, in words and pictures, from both natives and foreigners, including prominent Enlightenment figures and writers such as Voltaire and Nicolai. Apart from the royal building projects in Potsdam, the main focus of the exhibition lies on the establishment of luxury crafts under the protection of private manufacturing enterprises. The fourth section opens up the view of Potsdam to the period after the death of the king in 1786. The 46-year reign of Frederick the Great left its mark on Potsdam almost more than that of any other ruler, and the stamp of the king can still be felt to the present day. The assessment of Frederick ends in the present day. Contributions by contemporary artists invite the visitor to examine the role of Frederick the Great and the legacy of his age in Potsdam. It is hoped that this English catalogue will provide the reader with a selection of exhibits which will serve as an introduction to the subject of town planning under Frederick the Great.

The exhibition was made possible by the generous support of the many institutions and individuals who lent works. I should like to take this opportunity of thanking the museums, archives, libraries and private individuals for entrusting their works to us. I should also like to mention colleagues at universities and museums for their co-operation in numerous ways. To them, too, as to the other authors of the catalogue, we are particularly grateful.

The funding of the exhibition is linked to the overall funding of the museum. I should like to thank here the city of Potsdam and the state of Brandenburg, along with the numerous foundations, associations, businesses and private individuals who had a part in the creation of the exhibition, the German and English exhibition catalogues, and the accompanying educational materials.

The members of the project team were involved to a significant extent in the conception and realization of the exhibition and catalogue. I am particularly grateful to the two academic assistants and co-curators, Thomas Sander and Dr Ines Elsner. From the conservation side, the total planning of the exhibition and the care of all the exhibits was in the capable and tireless hands of Oliver Max Wenske. We should also like to thank the staff of the publishers, Hirmer Verlag of Munich, for their purposeful co-operation in the production of the German and English-language catalogues.

With the inaugural exhibition of the new Museum Quarter, we hope to demonstrate the new road which the Potsdam Museum – Forum für Kunst und Geschichte intends to take in the future.

Jutta Götzmann
Director of the Potsdam Museum – Forum für Kunst und Geschichte

Academic Advisory Council of the Museum

Prof. Dr. Dominik Bartmann
Stiftung Stadtmuseum, Berlin
Dr. Ingeborg Becker
Bröhan-Museum, Berlin
Prof. Dr. Monika Flacke
Stiftung Deutsches Historisches
Museum, Berlin
Dr. Jürgen Luh
Stiftung Preußische Schlösser und Gärten
Berlin-Brandenburg, Potsdam

Prof. Dr. Ralf Pröve
Universität Potsdam
Frühneuzeitzentrum Potsdam
Prof. Dr. Matthias Puhle
Kulturhistorisches Museum, Magdeburg
Prof. Dr. Luise Schorn-Schütte
Goethe-Universität Frankfurt am Main
FB Neuere Allgemeine Geschichte,
Frühe Neuzeit

Prof. Dr. Gisela Weiß
Hochschule für Technik, Wirtschaft und
Kultur Leipzig, FB Medien
Dr. Kurt Winkler
Haus der Brandenburgisch Preußischen
Geschichte, Potsdam

Lenders

Bayreuth, Bayerische Verwaltung der
staatlichen Schlösser, Gärten und Seen,
Neues Schloss
Berlin, Akademie der Künste, Kunst-
sammlung (AdK)
Berlin, Dieter Brusberg, Kunsthandel
GmbH
Berlin, Freie Universität Berlin, Univer-
sitätsbibliothek
Berlin, Geheimes Staatsarchiv, Stiftung
Preußischer Kulturbesitz (GStA)
Berlin, Potsdam, Seidel und Sohn,
Kunsthandel
Berlin, Staatliche Museen zu Berlin,
Stiftung Preußischer Kulturbesitz,
Kupferstichkabinett

Berlin, Staatsbibliothek zu Berlin, Stiftung
Preußischer Kulturbesitz
Berlin, Stiftung Deutsches Historisches
Museum (DHM)
Berlin, Stiftung Stadtmuseum Berlin
GmbH (SSMB)
Berlin, Privatleihgeber
Berlin, Holger Timm
Bremen, Privatleihgeber
Eichenzell, Hessische Hausstiftung,
Archiv Schloss Fasanerie
Eichenzell, Hessische Hausstiftung,
Museum Schloss Fasanerie
Frankfurt am Main, Museumsstiftung
Post und Telekommunikation (MSPT)

Münster, LWL Landesmuseum für Kunst
und Kulturgeschichte, Porträtarchiv
Diepenbroick
Potsdam, Brandenburgisches Landes-
hauptarchiv (BLHA)
Potsdam, E.ON edis AG
Potsdam, Katrin von Lehmann
Potsdam, Kiki Gebauer
Potsdam, Privatleihgeber
Potsdam, Sibylla Weisweiler
Potsdam Stiftung »Großes Waisenhaus zu
Potsdam«
Potsdam, Stiftung Preußische Schlösser
und Gärten Berlin-Brandenburg (SPSG)
Potsdam, Julia Theek
Potsdam, Anna Werkmeister

Authors

AB   Dr. Alexandra Bauer
MD   Mathias Deinert
IE   Dr. Ines Elsner
JG   Dr. Jutta Götzmann
SH   Saskia Hüneke
SK   Dr. Silke Kamp

KK   Dr. Käthe Klappenbach
JM   Dr. Jörg Meiner
BM   Dr. Birgit Möckel
TS   Thomas Sander
RS   René Schreiter
OMW   Oliver Max Wenske

Essays

Veduta ideata

The Alter Markt in Potsdam as the starting point and climax of Frederician urban design

'His gloriously reigning Majesty has chosen to pay special attention to making this city beautiful and its inhabitants happy.'

The Alter Markt is currently undergoing a renaissance of its Frederician composition. More than 10,000 citizens attended the topping-out ceremony for the Potsdam Landtag (state parliament) on 24 November 2011. It is being built on the ground plan of Frederick II's city palace and it is also very much based on the architectural language of forms used by its designer Georg Wenzeslaus von Knobelsdorff. The bidding competition for the plots on the Alte Fahrt has also been settled, and so too therefore has the development of the Alter Markt's southwest side. The projects include the reconstruction of Palais Barberini on Humboldtstrasse, which was originally built as 'Bürgerpalais' (citizen palace) for Frederick II by Georg Christian Unger and Carl von Gontard, two architects from Bayreuth. After the refurbishment of the Altes Rathaus (Old City Hall) and the Knobelsdorffhaus is complete, the buildings on the square's eastern side will shine in renewed splendour, and, housing the inaugural exhibition about Frederick II, they will give the Potsdam Museum a new home.

Frederick the Great's architecture, which once transformed Potsdam's historic centre into one of the most beautiful European Baroque squares, has returned to our attention again today. That itself is reason enough to look back at urban development between the time when the most significant member of the Hohenzollern dynasty acceded to the throne in 1740 and his death in 1786, and to ask how the genesis of this unique square took shape using specific exemplars from architectural history as models.

Urban development between 1740 and 1786

The king was intensely interested in European architecture and architectural theory, even as crown prince. This is confirmed by an exchange with Georg Wenzeslaus von Knobelsdorff, and

by his contact to the Venetian Count Francesco Algarotti from 1739. The latter acted as an important partner for correspondence and conversation, and also as someone who exposed the king to books and engravings. Frederick the Great's library is known to have contained more than 40 works on architecture, including several architectural treatises.

Immediately after ascending to the throne in 1740, Frederick II started by having Monbijou Palace and Charlottenburg

Palace extended by Knobelsdorff. Even while the construction phase was still ongoing in Berlin, he started his next ambitious project, namely expanding Potsdam to create a second residence with display functions. The fact that the king put so much energy and passion into extending the City Palace and into the new summer residence of Sanssouci was probably because he far preferred Potsdam to his main residence of Berlin, even in the early years of his reign. His architectural endeavours began on the Alter Markt in 1744 with the remodelling of his father's former palace. When Frederick came to the throne, the City Palace consisted of a three-storey corps de logis, emphasized by two corner risalits and a central one, as well as of two lower wings. The courtyard was bordered by a low gallery building with the centrally located Fortuna portal that led to the Alter Markt. The extension of the suite of rooms to the west of the marble hall, which was designated for guests, and the extension of the eastern wing were followed by extensive works on the exterior and finally the completion of the garden front in 1752.

The transformation of the City Palace into a prestige residence, based on designs by Georg Wenzeslaus von Knobelsdorff, was also very popular among Frederick's contemporaries. The French philosopher and writer Voltaire, who like no other embodied the spirit of the Enlightenment and free thinking, came to the Prussian court in 1750 and described the new era under Frederick II: 'His father had inhabited a scruffy house in Potsdam; Frederick turned it into a palace. Potsdam became a pretty town. Berlin expanded; the people started getting to know the pleasantries of life that the late king had paid very little attention to. [...] Things were constantly changing: Sparta was transformed into Athens.'

Starting in 1748 Frederick also focused on the development of Potsdam as a town by constructing new townhouses. The king's own designs demonstrate that he paid special attention to the appearance of the façade to match his personal tastes. Hans-Joachim Giersberg fittingly called them 'cabinet orders in the form of drawings'. The refurbishment of the residence in Potsdam was followed, until the outbreak of the Seven Years' War, by the further transformation of the Alter Markt into a square with an Italian ambience. The king entrusted Knobelsdorff with the subsequent commissions too, thus for example for the building at 10 Brauerstrasse, which is now called the 'Knobelsdorffhaus' and is part of the museum complex. Two years later, in 1752, Knobelsdorff applied the specifications of a Roman palace to the new building at 4 Alter Markt, which was to become a pastor's house and school.

The north side of the Alter Markt was home to St Nicholas's Church, which had been designed by Philipp Gerlach between 1721 and 1724 under Frederick William I. Between 1752 and 1755 Frederick had a Roman high-Baroque porch built on its southern end, whose façade faces the Alter Markt. The two-storey façade was elaborately structured by columns and pilasters, while round gables and pediments contributed to the façade's rich ornamentation. The upper central field was adorned by a fresco by the painter Charles-Amédée-Philippe van Loo. The projecting arcades around the church nave were used as market stalls. The actual square of the Alter Markt was re-levelled and given a central obelisk measuring more than 16 metres in height. Designed by Knobelsdorff and built between 1753 and 1755, it depicted Roman senators on the sides of the pedestal, while the lower end of the shaft depicted four marble tondos between Egyptian sphinxes. The tondos feature the profiles of the Great Elector as well as of the kings Frederick I, Frederick William I and Frederick II. In the canon of forms of Roman antiquity, Frederick thus placed himself in the line of his ancestors and revealed himself to posterity as the square's donor and founder.

Old City Hall and Palais Barberini – start of construction and dissemination in the visual media

One of the highlights of Frederick's projects for the square is undoubtedly the (by then) fourth town hall opposite the royal residence, with which the architects Jan Bouman and Christian Ludwig Hildebrandt were commissioned in 1753. It replaced Pierre Gayette's 1720 timber-frame building constructed under Frederick William I. The new building was made necessary by the increased legal and administrative tasks required. It was the king who commissioned this building and the neighbouring townhouses, and not, as was the case for the much-quoted model, the City Hall in Amsterdam, the municipal authorities. The attempt to expand the width of the building by incorporating the neighbouring property failed because of the stubbornness of the latter's owner Martin Windelbandt. Frederick's brief to base the project on the design of a northern Italian palace façade and to combine it with a round tambour led to the use of a more massive substructure. The result in turn was a reduction in the much-needed interior space. It was typical of Frederick's approach to his city improvement project that he left the old wings of the previous building standing behind the new building, and had the wing facing the road renovated only in 1775, when it was already in a somewhat rundown state.

Frederick aimed the main focus of the new building at the façade facing the Alter Markt, instead of at the structure as a whole with a functional interior room layout. This is something he did with several other buildings too. A colossal Corinthian order structures the façade into seven bays. The engaged columns in the attic section are continued as pilaster strips and adorned with allegorical sandstone figures. They were made by Johann Gottlieb Heymüller and embody the virtues of watchfulness, steadfastness, abundance, justice, trade and prudence. The tambour is fitted with a stepped dome and supplements the figure scheme with the gilded lead statue of Atlas designed by Benjamin Giese. The original fell on to the Alter Markt in 1776. On the king's instruction it was replaced by a copy of beaten copper.

The City Hall receives favourable mention in contemporary architecture and travel descriptions of Potsdam. Friedrich Nicolai, the son of a bookseller family, who himself wrote in favour of the Enlightenment, devoted himself to a first detailed description of the City Hall façade in his *Beschreibung der königlichen Residenzstädte Berlin und Potsdam* ('Description of the royal residence cities of Berlin and Potsdam'), published in 1769. The precise naming of the internal room layout also goes back to him. Nicolai compared the previous building on the Alter Markt to the one in Amsterdam, presumably agreeing with Bellaminte, who did the same in *Das Itzt-blühende Potsdam* ('The Now-Blossoming Potsdam') in 1727. In 1788 he praised the Old City Hall as the most beautiful example of urban architecture in the *Teutsche Merkur,* a monthly magazine for the upper middle classes published between 1773 and 1789: 'The market square is home to the Italian-style Catholic church and has an obelisk as its centre which looks very good [...]. It is the location of the City Hall, the most delicate and noble building in the whole of Potsdam.'

Sixteen years after its completion, the Frederician design of the Alter Markt came to a monumental conclusion on the southern side, in the form of Potsdam's Palais Barberini. Frederick merged two properties, which had previously been in the possession of Potsdam citizens Reckloff and Berckholz, and had a pair of semi-detached houses built on the site in 1771/72. One new feature for Potsdam was the number of storeys. Instead of the customary two to four storeys, Palais

Fig. 3 Andrea Palladio, *Design for the Palazzo Angarano in Vicenza*, ground plan and façade, in: Palladio 1581, p. 75, Berlin, SBB PK

Barberini was given five storeys. The architects Carl von Gontard and Georg Christian Unger were both commissioned with the project.

The façade is characterized by a projecting five-bay central risalit, which is framed by four-bay wings. In contrast to the five-storey wings, which were all fitted with a mezzanine above the first and second main floors, the central risalit was a generous three-storey design. In line with the classical canon of forms, the façade featured the Doric order with engaged columns for the ground floor, the Ionic engaged columns for the first floor and the Corinthian pilaster arrangement for the second floor.

Manger's architectural history of Potsdam is an important source for attributing the decorative features. According to this work, Potsdam sculptor Nathanael Eppen and his assistants produced capitals and vases, while stucco plasterer and faience manufacturer Constantin Philipp Georg Sartori was responsible for the remaining decor (Manger 1789/90, vol. 2, p. 365).

With regard to the building's commissioning and use, the term 'Immediatbau', coined by Astrid Fick, is more appropriate than the much used 'Bürgerpalais' ('citizen palace'), as it allows for the fact that the king largely took on the costs and determined the architectural appearance, which meant he could fulfil his display needs 'immediately' (in the sense of 'without intermediaries') and also in the 'immediate' surroundings of his residence along central streets and squares. The citizenry were then given the finished building without regard for how they would use the finished space.

We owe the fact that we have an idea of the Frederician design of the Alter Markt in part to its depiction in visual media. For Frederick, an enlightened monarch, renown did not just come from warfare, but also from nurturing art, science and architecture. Potsdam's development with magnificent palaces, townhouses and elaborate squares of European format, was not just a symbol of his own greatness, but also an expression of his country's ability. Large picture cycles, which captured the dazzling urban development in images and were in turn used as models for graphic depictions that enjoyed widespread circulation, were produced in the service of courtly prestige.

Immediately after the completion of the Alter Markt in the 1770s, picturesque vedutas emerged, such as those by Johann Friedrich Meyer and Carl Christian Wilhelm Baron. Extensive cycles of prints were also published, such as those by Andreas Ludwig Krüger, Meyer's son-in-law and talented Potsdam-based draughtsman and later director of the Baucomptoir. The king had Meyer's and Baron's vedutas hung in the guest

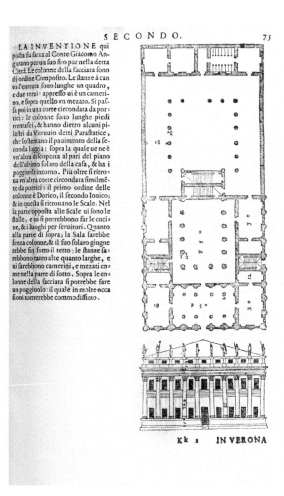

accommodation in the New Chambers of Sanssouci and used them as 'ideal and authorized hints on how to read the city of Potsdam' (Oesterreich 1773, p. 33; Becker 2005, p. 222). Thus the paintings in the New Chambers include the artistic version of the Frederician design of the square created by Carl Christian Wilhelm Baron in 1772 (fig. 1). The veduta directs the gaze of the beholder across the crowded market place, which is characterized by stalls and performing artists, to the north side of the square with St Nicholas's church in the middle. Slightly hidden behind the obelisk in the square can be seen the Roman-style façade projection built under Frederick, which was laconically known in popular parlance as the 'Vorhemdchen' (lit. 'little shirt hanging in front', but perhaps more appropriately: 'apron'). In the left foreground of the picture is the adjacent west side of the Alter Markt with the boldly capped theatre wing of the City Palace, and to the right the lively east side of the square with the Old City Hall. Between the church and the

City Hall can be seen the heavily foreshortened façade of the pastor's residence and schoolhouse belonging to the parish of St Nicholas.

If we now turn, as beholders, away from the frontal perspective of St Nicholas's church to the right, from the level of Schlossstrasse we have the approximate, slightly raised standpoint occupied by Andreas Ludwig Krüger to capture the east side of the Alter Markt with the City Hall, obelisk and Palais Barberini in his ink and wash drawing of 1775 (fig. 2). Of this view too, which shifts the less crowded square away from the beholder somewhat, there exist numerous coloured and non-coloured variations, including raree-show pictures. The Baroque 'apron' of St Nicholas's church can now be seen on the left-hand edge of the picture, while the centre ground is determined by the elaborate façades of the Old City Hall and the Palais Barberini. The fact that both on this sheet and on the painted originals by Baron and Meyer the Italian designs are easily recognizable was doubtless also intended by the king, who emphasized the selection of Italian architectural exemplars to his secretary and 'reader' Henri Alexandre de Catt , and at the same time pointed to all the money he had spent in order to make 'his Potsdam' a pleasant place (De Catt 1940, p. 53).

The European models for the buildings on the Alter Markt

In his standard work on Potsdam architecture, *Potsdamer Baukunst,* Friedrich Mielke pointed out that there was never a self-contained Italian quarter with predominantly Italian inhabitants, but nevertheless 'in the immediate vicinity of the City Palace [there were] eight imitations of Italian façades, which characterized the image of the Alter Markt and the frontage of the adjoining Humboldtstrasse and Schlossstrasse'. Including the Lustgarten, Christian Wendland lists fourteen Italianate buildings. In the Potsdam City Palace and the townhouse at no. 10 Brauerstrasse (the 'Knobelsdorffhaus') the formal vocabulary of English Neo-Palladianism was still the determining factor. The stimuli here came from Knobelsdorff, who, doubtless together with the king, had studied Colen Campbell's *Vitruvius Britannicus* of 1731, a copy of which was in the royal library. Contact with Lord Burlington in England was provided by Algarotti, who is known to have introduced the king to a Palladio book and drawings of English Palladian buildings. For all of the remaining design of the Alter Markt, however, the models were provided by Italian buildings of the sixteenth to eighteenth centuries. On 27 April 1758, Frederick said to de Catt: 'To Potsdam, to Potsdam, that's where I need

to go if I want to be happy. When you see this city, you will certainly like it. In my father's day it was a wretched little place; if he were to come back now, he would certainly not recognize his town, so much have I done to beautify it. I have selected the plans for the most beautiful buildings in Europe, mainly in Italy, and am having them executed on a small scale in accordance with my means. The proportions have been meticulously followed. All of my buildings please the people, as you will be able to convince yourself. I confess that I like building and ornamenting very much.' (De Catt 1940, p. 53).

Which individual buildings Frederick selected, and how they were adapted to conditions in Potsdam, whether as copy, imitation, or as new creation, has occupied scholars from Manger to the present (cf. most recently Becker 2005). It is doubtless important in this connexion to bear in mind that Frederick never copied a building in its entirety, in other words he took into account the ground plan and elevation, the size and the proportions, and thus all the factors that were crucial for architectural harmony on the one hand, and on the other for function and use. Frederick frequently oriented himself by façade, designing more a backdrop than an architecturally thought-through building.

Thus for the rebuilding of the Old City Hall, and years later, the house at no. 4 Humboldtstrasse, the king was inspired by Andrea Palladio, whose architectural treatise *I quattro libri dell'architettura* had been brought to his attention by Francesco Algarotti (fig. 3). The translations of this work into French, English and German, which had already been made in the seventeenth and early eighteenth centuries, are proof of the extensive reception of this theoretical discourse, at the heart of which is the doctrine of proportions going back to Vitruvius, which determines the sequences of rooms and their symmetrical arrangements. The catalogue of works on architecture in Frederick II's libraries shows that he possessed the French edition of 1727. He also had access to Vitruvius's ten-volume architectural treatise in a French edition of 1648.

Specifically, Frederick chose as his model for the Potsdam City Hall the palazzo of Count Giacomo Angarano, which Andrea Palladio had designed for the count's plot of land in Vicenza in 1564, but which was never built. The king wanted to incorporate the house next-door on the right, which belonged to a baker named Windelbandt, into a nine-bay façade, but was unsuccessful. On a smaller plot, he tried to adapt the proportions to Potsdam conditions, in which he certainly succeeded as far as the façade design with its colossal orders and superimposed attic storey went, but which in combination

with a tambour and dome led, as Mielke put it, to the building looking top-heavy. We can see from the example of the Old City Hall how Frederick quoted Palladio, while ignoring the architect's basic idea, because it did not create any harmonious proportions through a balance of interior and exterior, of ground plan and elevation.

Frederick often proceeded along set-piece lines when choosing his models. Palladio's architecture, which always defines the building as a unit, was reduced by the king to its façade, which he combined with the tambour as a reminder of the Amsterdam City Hall and the Potsdam predecessor. The dome motif, by contrast, is borrowed from the Pantheon in Rome. The orientation to the Amsterdam City Hall, as handed down by Heinrich Ludwig Manger and Friedrich Nicolai, is derived from its use as an administrative building, and is based in the upper segment of the building on the tambour motif and the figure programme of Atlas and Virtue depictions. Even

though the Amsterdam City Hall represented a more complex programme of 'good government' and 'universal peace', an association with the Potsdam City hall vis-à-vis the royal residence may not have been without significance.

From the loyal address to Frederick II on the occasion of the rebuilding of the City Hall in 1753, we learn that: '[…] His Royal Majesty in Prussia, our most gracious lord, had this splendid City Hall rebuilt at his own expense by the royal Ober-Kastellan Johann Bouman as an ornament for the city and to strengthen justice' (BLHA, Rep. 19, no. 3250).

Then follows the listing of a canon of virtues attributed to the ruler, emphasizing his courage, his wisdom, his magnanimity and his justice, and likewise his tireless diligence and his attention to the best interests of his subjects: good government was guaranteed exclusively by the *virtutes* of the monarch. These also included building, for 'regardless of the heavy expenses involved in the military campaigns', Frederick devoted large sums of money to the building of 'most gracious palaces in order to multiply the nourishment of the inhabitants'.

For the south side of the Alter Markt, nos. 5/6 Humboldt-strasse, the model was provided by the Palazzo Barberini in Rome, which also gave the building, erected in 1771/72, its name. Astrid Fick has already noted that the imposing structure was among the largest buildings in Potsdam to have been built on the basis of a foreign model. The 'exemplar' function of the Palazzo Barberini in Rome, which was built between 1625 and 1700, was demonstrated by Krüger in 1779. As was already the case with the Old City Hall, it was not the whole structure designed by the Roman architects Carlo Maderno, Francesco Borromini and Gianlorenzo Bernini: here too Frederick only had part of the building, specifically the central risalit of the front elevation, adapted for Potsdam.

'The two wings are linked to the risalit, and are composed to accompany it. One might fairly describe the building as a free translation.' (Krüger 1779). Unlike the Old City Hall, the building in its totality was developed homogeneously from its exemplar. The ground-plan situation, which in Rome is characterized by a horseshoe-shaped layout with a set-back central tract, was changed at the request of the king in favour of a continuous façade. The intermediary in this case may have been Gontard, who had doubtless seen the architectural original on his trip to Rome in 1754/55.

As is well known, the king also took his inspiration from the Italian architects Michele Sanmicheli and Ferdinando Fuga, knowledge of whom he acquired via engravings by Piranesi. In 1752 he instructed his architect Knobelsdorff to provide St Nicholas's church and the neighbouring building (school and pastor's house) with façades on the model of buildings by Ferdinando Fuga in Rome. Thus for the façade porch which the church acquired between 1752 and 1755 an adaptation of the façade of Santa Maria Maggiore in Rome, designed by Fuga twelve years earlier (fig. 4), was required. The frontage of the neighbouring pastor's house and school was an obvious imitation of the façade of the Palazzo della Consultà in Rome, which had been built between 1732 and 1734 to plans by Ferdinando Fuga for the papal chancellery and cavalry barracks.

The idea of placing an obelisk in the centre of the Alter Markt also goes back to the concept of a Roman *piazza*. The king may have had access to eighteenth-century paintings or engravings of the Piazza San Pietro, for example the painting by Giovanni Paolo Pannini (c. 1725). Likewise, he may also have known engravings or medallions depicting the Piazza del Popolo.

As he expounded to de Catt, Frederick II chose for the Alter Markt 'the plans of the most beautiful buildings in Europe, in particular in Italy' and had them implemented in Potsdam in accordance with his means and the local situation. On the one hand, he paid tribute to the great European architects by realizing their buildings as a collection of important reference works. On the other hand, he often interfered with the harmony of complex buildings by reducing them to their main façades; at the same time there was almost always a change of use, with princely palaces being turned into dwellings for craftsmen and small tradesmen. The concept of the *veduta ideata*, coined for the cityscapes of Canaletto and Piranesi, can, as suggested by Becker too, be transferred to one of the most beautiful squares in Europe, which came about as the ideal and at the same time artificial composition of its creator.

JUTTA GÖTZMANN

Select Bibliography

Palladio 1581; Palladio repr. 1726; Oesterreich 1773; Millenet 1776; Krüger 1779; Manger 1789/90, vol. 2; De Catt 1940; Mielke 1981; De Catt repr. 1954; Giersberg 1982; Giersberg 1986; Heller 1987b; Klünner 1991; Hoeftmann/Noack 1992; Nicolai repr., 1993; Palladio repr. 1993; Fick 2000; Bellamintes repr. 2001; Wendland 2002; Becker 2005; Maruhn/Schmidt 2006; Kitschke 2008; Felgendreher 2011

Fig. 5 Detail of *Silk 'Peking' from a bedroom in the Marquis d'Argens apartment,* Neues Palais, Potsdam, presumably made in Isaac Joël's factory in Glienicke, c. 1768, Potsdam, SPSG

The Wallpaper Factory of the 'Protected Jew' Isaac Levin Joël

The silk industry in Potsdam under Frederick II

Isaac Levin Joël's wallpaper factory in the former electoral hunting lodge of Glienicke Palace was one of the most successful factories in Potsdam during the reign of Frederick II. In addition to simple waxcloth, oilcloth and linen wall hangings were also primed, printed and painted in Glienicke, while the high-quality silks were delivered pre-dyed and were only painted in Joël's factory. These fabrics were of great significance for Prussian interior decoration during the late eighteenth century, both in royal palaces as well as in the palaces of the aristocracy and the upper middle classes.

From the start of his reign Frederick II furthered silk culture and silk production in Prussia, an undertaking already initiated by his predecessors. Experts were imported and trained by attracting them with privileges, the production of raw silk was promoted and the manufacture and sale of silk goods favoured. The goal of this intensive royal support was to cover the domestic demand for silk goods with domestic products. In addition, the high quality of the products was intended to increase the country's reputation and make a successful export industry possible. At the royal behest, the newly created Fifth Department of the *Generaldirektorium*, responsible for trade, factory and manufacture issues and run by minister Samuel von Marschall, devoted itself with particular intensity to the silk industry. Just three months after his accession, Frederick

urged the minister to push forward the relocation of silk makers from Italy and to force through the establishment of new factories. In 1746 the king praised Marschall's efforts to relocate silk makers and set up factories, and added: '[...] what I recommend to you most strongly now are the silk factories. I want you to give all your hard work to establishing and multiplying them, as they are now my main focus [...].'

After the Second Silesian War this state promotion gradually showed some success. It was not just the number of businesses and their sizes that were greatly increased; so too were the technical abilities to weave different fabrics.

Silk making and the silk trade in Potsdam

The vast majority of the newly founded silk factories were set up in Berlin, where this luxury industry established itself during the reign of Frederick II. However, the entrepreneurs in the king's residence of Potsdam also profited from royal assistance to the silk industry. First, the existing factories were strengthened, then, in the 1750s, a few new factories and branches of Berlin-based companies were opened. Generally speaking, the profile of Potsdam's economy was largely shaped by Jewish entrepreneurs. This is especially true of the silk industry, whose most important representatives in Potsdam were David Hirsch, Isaak Bernhard and Moses Ries, all members of the Jewish community.

At the behest of King Frederick William I, the 'protected Jew' David Hirsch from Berlin had already opened a velvet factory in Potsdam in 1730. Thanks to a twelve-year privilege, which gave the business a monopoly position in the manufacture of velvet in the royal lands, the factory in Nauensche Strasse prospered, even in economically difficult times. Masters and journeymen with technical skills in the production of velvet were called to Brandenburg from Hamburg, Holland and Copenhagen, while the apprentices were provided by the military orphanage in Potsdam. In the following years David Hirsch expanded his business with a silk factory (1732) and by producing wool and silk plush (1733). When the exclusive privilege for velvet production ended in 1742, Frederick II extended it by a further ten years, '[...] since H. M. is very happy with the success of the velvet and plush manufacture to date and public interest requires that it be supported [...]'.

However, after just four years the king demanded a significantly increased production from his protégé, which the latter could only have implemented with massive financial assistance. As a result, Frederick II chose the less expensive option

of setting up a second velvet factory, thereby breaking the monopoly David Hirsch had held as the only manufacturer of this fabric in the country. The fact that he also initially wanted to build this factory in Potsdam is evidence that the city on the Havel had already become a centre of velvet production. Since, however, no entrepreneur in Potsdam was willing to run such a factory, the trimmings manufacturer and court purveyor Friedrich Blume obtained permission to build a velvet factory in Berlin in 1746. Among the conditions laid down in writing was one that the factory in Berlin was not allowed to limit the sales of the Potsdam factory, that Blume was not allowed to poach any of Hirsch's employees, and that both factories were to be considered on equal terms regarding supplies for the court. In a 1770 report, Hirsch described the economic difficulties that he experienced because of the king's breach of the legal arrangements and the direct competition he confronted as a result. These problems were made even worse by the consequences of the Seven Years' War and the establishment of a third velvet factory in 1765. This factory was run by Potsdam-based manufacturer Moses Isaak, and was abandoned again just three years later.

While Potsdam had clearly established itself as the leading location for velvet manufacture at the behest of Frederick II, the silk factories played a subordinate role. Only the two businesses newly established by Heinrich Stiphout, which were later taken over by Isaak Bernhard and Moses Ries, achieved a certain significance; however, they never matched Berlin in size and influence. Heinrich Stiphout, a Dutchman, held a special position among the predominantly Jewish and French entrepreneurs of the silk industry at that time. Enticed by subsidies, the trained silk knitter came to Potsdam in 1750 in order to open a damask and silk factory. Just four years later this factory was in decline, but continued to receive a striking amount of royal support. One reason for Frederick II's special interest in Stiphout's factory was probably the product range. If it was possible to produce heavy Dutch cloth, Dutch damask and English moirés in Potsdam, then it would no longer be necessary to import silks of this kind. In 1758 the successful Berlin-based silk entrepreneur Isaak Bernhard took over Stiphout's factory in Potsdam, as a trial at first, but after the peace of 1763, it was transferred to him completely.

In 1748 the 'protected Jew' Moses Ries from Berlin, the son-in-law of the court jeweller Veitel Ephraim, founded a damask and gros de Tours factory in Potsdam, which mainly focused on exporting to Poland, Russia and Hungary. When he took over the velvet factory in Berlin from Christian Friedrich

Blume's heirs, he became one of the leading silk entrepreneurs during Frederick II's reign.

Under Frederick II, the manufacturers in Potsdam generally benefited more from state support than those in Berlin, which was interpreted as a sign of the king's preference for the former. The city of his residence was intended to impress not just with buildings, parks and artworks, but also with a strong economy. For all the massive support, only velvet manufacturing became a success story for Potsdam. Silk production remained secondary. Trade in silk also only played a subordinate role in Potsdam. Until the late eighteenth century there was no independent guild for cloth and silk dealers. The few entrepreneurs in Potsdam who dealt in such manufactured goods were registered in Berlin.

Silks for the New Palace

The centre of the silk industry in the eighteenth century was Berlin. The factories there had made so much artistic and technical progress since the 1760s that they were able to make 'rich fabrics'. These heavy silk fabrics, embroidered with silk, silver, gold or chenille threads, attained a quality that could compete with the leading French products of that period. This too was a development that Frederick II was substantially responsible for. It is indicative of the king's personal commitment to his preferred residence of Potsdam that he chose the New Palace in Sanssouci Park, rather than one of his Berlin residences, for a kind of showroom where he collected samples of the high-quality fabrics from Berlin. Many silk fabrics in the form of wall-hangings, furniture coverings and curtains still survive there to this day. Most of them can be attributed to factories in Berlin. This is shown by the examinations conducted on the decorative silks of the eighteenth century in the Prussian palaces by the Prussian Palaces and Gardens Foundation to mark Frederick II's tercentenary in 2012. The results are to be published in an inventory catalogue. The royal apartment alone has five richly embroidered eighteenth-century fabrics that can be attributed to the leading Berlin-based factories of Girard & Michelet, the Baudouin brothers, Isaak Berhard, and Puis (fig. 7). Two further interior fabrics are marked by a signature as works by the silk factory run by the Baudouin brothers: a silk lampas embroidered with silver and chenille threads from the Jagdkammer in the Oberes Fürstenquartier and the palmette-pattern red damask in the Tressenzimmer of the Unteres Fürstenquartier. Both the rich fabrics as well as the plainer damasks in the New Palace came from the local factories supported by Frederick II. Contemporaries felt this was particularly worth mentioning because silk fabrics of such quality were usually of French origin in the eighteenth century. In his *Beschreibung der königlichen Residenzstadt Potsdam* ('Description of the royal residence of Potsdam'), Friedrich Nicolai named the manufacturers of the silk in many rooms in the New Palace, or he comments that they were 'from a factory in Berlin'. Anton Friedrich Büsching was also pleased about the high quality of the domestic silk production:

'For a patriot it is a great joy to hear that a large amount of the beautiful, precious things he sees in the New Palace were made by artists who live in Potsdam and Berlin. The rich, beautiful and precious fabrics with which so many rooms are decorated were made in the factories of Messrs Girard, Michelet and Bodevins in Berlin.'

In addition to the 'rich things' and the damasks, a third genre of interior textiles in the New Palace, which had received virtually no attention before, was also largely manufactured by domestic companies: the painted and printed wall hangings, which, according to the information in the earliest inventory log of 1784, could be found in a total of 52 rooms. While printed linen fabrics were only recorded in nine cases, the painted linen wallpapers were the most common, there being 24 of them. Painted silks were present in 19 rooms, and given their higher value, that is a large number. By far the largest percentage of rooms with printed or painted linen or silk fabrics were on the third floor of the New Palace. 39 of 41 simply furnished guest rooms and servants' rooms were wallpapered in this fashion. Their use in rooms of low status is indicative of the standing of these kinds of wallpaper. Their significance falls far behind the rich fabrics and the damasks. However, painted linen and silk wallpapers were also found in the apartments of the king's

siblings: the 'princess apartment', presumably designated for Frederick's sister Amalie, and the apartment meant for his brother Heinrich. In addition, a total of ten rooms in the Marquis d'Argens apartment on the ground floor of the New Palace, right next to the king's quarters, are also fitted with painted wallpapers, two of them in the form of oil paintings inserted in wall panels. It is demonstrated in these cases that the fabrics, known as 'Peckings' [sic] in contemporary inventories, were also deliberately integrated into richly decorated sequences of rooms. The vital aspect here was not their reputed character as an inexpensive and inferior *ersatz* for woven wall coverings, but their up-to-date quality and fashionable appeal. So-called 'Pekings', Chinoiserie wallpapers where rambling plants, leaves, flowers, birds and butterflies were painted on a light background, were extremely fashionable during the second half of the eighteenth century. The Prussian palaces of that era also had quite a few Chinoiserie wallpapers hung, for example the Chinese House in Sanssouci Park and the rooms of Frederick II's consort, Queen Elisabeth Christine, in Schönhausen Palace.

A wealth of documents from the years 1767–1769 survive for the fabric makers and wallpaper factories for the 'Pekings' of the New Palace. For the first time they can be matched with concrete rooms on the third floor of the New Palace. During two decorating operations, Girard & Michelet and Isaak Bernhard produced the fabrics for a total of 27 rooms, which were then painted by the Potsdam-based wallpaper factory of Isaac Joël and the Berlin-based competitor Sonnin & Bando. Unfortunately this matching only involves wallpapers that have not survived and whose patterns we do not know; where the fabrics and patterns survive, the documents do not. Since the contemporary quantities and accounts confirm that half the painting was done by Joël and half by Sonnin & Bando, it seems likely that the same is true for the rooms that are not documented. It is possible that there was originally a similar agreement about the fair distribution of all of the court's commissions, as is documented for David Hirsch's and Christian Friedrich Blume's silk factories.

The wallpaper factory of Potsdam-based 'protected Jew' Isaac Levin Joël

The evaluation of the documents about the decoration of the New Palace with painted silk and linen wallpapers throws new light on Isaac Levin Joël's factory in Potsdam. Probably born into a distinguished Jewish family of scholars in Halberstadt in 1712, he received the 'protection letter' that allowed him to live in Brandenburg-Prussia in 1734. In 1746 he was already based in Potsdam, because it was at this time that he founded an embroidery workshop in the king's military orphanage. According to the contract, the orphanage provided 50 girls and paid for their upkeep. In return the entrepreneur agreed to train the orphans. They learned to sew and embroider men's cuffs. In 1754 Joël requested permission for a 'private privilege', i.e. a monopoly for this kind of colourful embroidery. However, since a businessman named Guthmann in Berlin was making those kinds of goods too, and would therefore be disadvantaged, Joël was not granted the privilege.

Just three years earlier Joël had tried to obtain a concession for the production of waxcloth wallpapers. With a good sense for future trends and lucrative business, he must have recognized that this kind of wall covering was becoming increasingly popular among the aristocracy and the gentry and that waxcloth hangings had hitherto had to be imported at high prices from Saxony. Johann Friedrich Meyer, a painter from Potsdam who had learned the skill of painting waxcloth hang-

ings in Dresden, also requested a concession, but both were rejected in 1752. The attempts at this time mainly failed because no building could be made available to them, wallpaper manufacture needing more space than other enterprises. It was not until 1758 that things changed as a result of an intervention by the influential General Friedrich Bogislav von Tauentzien. As an advocate of Joël's plans for a factory, he persuaded Frederick II to let the businessman have the old Glienicke Palace near Potsdam as a production site. The location of the electoral hunting lodge on the Havel river, used as a military hospital for Potsdam's regiment since the reign of Frederick William I, and the courtyards and gardens, which were indispensable for drying the wallpapers, meant this venue had the ideal conditions for waxcloth production. Files from the years 1758 and 1760 confirm that the new factory was already producing a large selection of high-quality waxcloth wallpapers, and that the business had a flower painter, a figure painter and a gilder from Leipzig, the centre of waxcloth production at the time. In addition it had a printer, a silhouette painter and a linen weaver. Johann Carl Gottfried Jacobsson's descriptions in his *Schauplatz der Zeugmanufakturen in Deutschland* (1773) and those in *Peter Nathanael Sprengels Handwerke und Künste in Tabellen* (1777) illustrate the production of waxed-linen wallpapers in great detail. The necessary canvas was first stretched over a large frame with twine. If the wallpaper was ordered for a specific room, the canvas size was tailored to the height of the room and then the lengths were sewn together before mounting them on a frame. After that they were covered in paste, and after air-drying, with a foundation of resin-rich black soot and boiled oil. After that they were once again dried outside. This process took place in the summer because of the weather, while the winters were used for printing and painting. The simpler wallpapers were decorated using block printing. The stamps produced outlines and hatchings of the pattern, which were then painted and shaded with the help of lead white, while the more expensive ones were only painted (fig. 6). According to contemporary reports, specialities of Joël's factory manufacture included linen Chinoiserie wallpapers. That the factory also produced silk Chinoiserie wallpapers on a large scale was only discovered when the documents relating to the New Palace were evaluated. Unfortunately only two of the once plentiful painted silk wallpapers still survive. In addition to a typical Chinoiserie wall covering with birds and rambling plants in one of the bedrooms in the Marquis d'Argens apartment (fig. 5), there are two fragments with a similar floral pattern that were kept by for use in the event of a repair. As is the case of the three surviving eighteenth-century linen Chinoiserie wallpapers, also from the apartment of the Marquis d'Argens (fig. 8) and from Prince Heinrich's apartment, it cannot be said with certainty which wallpaper factory was responsible for their production.

As is confirmed by the extensive writings about painted wallpapers in Frederick II's new guest palace dating from the years 1767–1769, Joël's factory in Potsdam evidently shared its commissions with Sonnin & Bando (see above) in Berlin. Even their contemporaries emphasized that these two factories more or less held a monopoly:

'There is just a single waxcloth wallpaper factory in Berlin that was set up by Sonnin and Bando 18 to 20 years ago. [...] In addition there is a waxcloth and Pequin [sic] wallpaper factory in Glieneke near Potsdam, which belongs to the Jew Isaac Joël.'

There are numerous documents that comment on the competition between the two businesses. In many cases Sonnin & Bando turned against Joël, who was evidently more successful. They sued him on account of his branch in Berlin, which Joël had run from the outset and for which he got a concession in 1774. In addition the files on the decoration of the royal palaces contain a letter from Sonnin & Bando, dated 18 February 1767 and addressed to Carl von Gontard, which says that the manufacturers from Berlin feared that Joël, because of his presence in Potsdam and therefore his proximity to the king, could achieve advantages for himself: 'Your Highness will be so gracious and will not forget us when new orders are to be commissioned again, as we are not so present as Herr Joel is and cannot therefore seek you out as he can, as he is in loco.'

This request was backed up by the dispatch of smoked Pomeranian geese. Frederick II's invoices confirm that the concerns of the businessmen from Berlin were justified. While 13 payments were made to Isaac Joël between 1768 and 1770, the Sonnin & Bando company is listed just once.

The long and positive relationship between Isaac Levin Joël and Frederick II, King of Prussia, which could not be taken for granted by a Jewish entrepreneur, ended with Joël's death in 1785, one year before the death of the king. Joël's workshops and factories for embroidery and wallpapers were among the

leading companies in Potsdam in the eighteenth century and significantly contributed to its economic growth. Joël was one of the few Jewish entrepreneurs working in Potsdam who also lived there; most of the others lived in Berlin. For that reason the story of the wallpaper factory is very much a success story for Potsdam. Joël's sons continued to run the factory with success until the nineteenth century. Wallpaper deliveries for the royal buildings of Frederick II's successors, such as for the Kavalierhaus (1790) and the Weisses Haus (1796) in the Neuer Garten, for the boxes of the royal theatre in Potsdam (1794) and Paretz Palace (1797/1798) confirm this late phase of the wallpaper manufacture, which has not yet been studied in any great detail.

SUSANNE EVERS

Select Bibliography

Jacobsson 1773–1776; Sprengels 1777; Nicolai 1786; Schneider 1862; Schmoller/Hintze 1892; Stengel 1958; Hofmann 1969; Straubel 1995; Thümmler 1998; Herzfeld 2001; Büsching 2006; Meier 2007; Beckert 2008; Schendel 2008; Evers 2012; Evers/Zitzmann, currently being printed.

Fig. 9 Johann August Nahl, *Wall mirror*,
c. 1745, Fulda, HH (cat. 28)

Nature and Ornament

The furniture for Frederick the Great

'The king's good taste spread across the nation.'

Among all the artistic epochs of court furniture in the Kingdom of Prussia, only the period under Frederick the Great managed to be remembered by posterity by a fixed term based on the ruler's name. What was standard in France and other European monarchies in the eighteenth and nineteenth centuries was the exception in Prussia. However, it is by no means the case that only Frederick the Great involved himself in promoting art and culture, thereby also intervening in the designs of luxury furniture, in a way that this personalized naming was possible only for his era. His grandfather Frederick I of Prussia significantly contributed to the direction of court furniture at the start of the eighteenth century with the groundbreaking appointment of Schlüter and Eosander. Even before 1786 the future Frederick William II as heir to the throne paved the way for the rapid development of a specifically Prussian early Neoclassicism after his uncle's death by sponsoring David Roentgen and appointing Erdmannsdorff and Langhans. For the 'long' nineteenth century too, there are two rulers, Frederick William IV and William II (Kaiser Wilhelm II), whose personal and direct involvement (not least with their own designs, forceful purchasing policies and specific support) influenced both the quality and the design of court furniture. During the reign of Frederick William III, the commissioning of Karl Friedrich Schinkel to furnish the court had a significant and lasting effect on the interior-design style of that period. The fact that only Frederick the Great managed to obtain the honour of having a style named after him is probably due to the fact that posterity doubtless added his incredible influence on art and handicrafts to his outstanding political significance and his strong

personal regime. The epochal magnitude of a political body of work is closely associated with that of the *gesamtkunstwerk* or total artistic work. Heinrich Ludwig Manger (1789/90), a chronicler from Potsdam, considered Frederick II to be the 'great leader' of this development of artistic life in Potsdam that spanned four decades; for Nicolai the king's 'good taste' was also the pointer for the liberal and applied arts of the Prussian 'nation'. The king's presence was considered the sole engine of this development. If he were not acting in such a capacity, the quality of art and handicrafts in the city and the country would necessarily also stagnate.

It is, however, invariably only the furniture in the palaces that was essentially shaped by the ruler's influence. The furniture made for the bourgeoisie and the aristocracy is, on the whole, formally and in detail merely derivative of the specimens at court. While this can be confirmed quite well in the nineteenth century for objects whose origin and date of manufacture are known, it is less obvious for the furniture that did not furnish palaces during the time of Frederick the Great. The furniture of the citizenry generally possessed less elaborate ornamentation, and it may also have been more conservative in appearance. This assumption is refuted by Anton Balthasar König's report (1799), a document characterized by its critical attitude to culture. Commenting in retrospect on Berlin during the reign of Frederick the Great, he concluded that all the citizens, even master craftsmen, 'got rid of old, enduring, fixed household items meant for generations […] because it got on their nerves.' The creations of 'the great and rich […] set the patterns' for the new, modern 'meubles' bought on 'credit'. It could therefore very well be that some of the Frederician pieces in public collections or on the art market, which cannot be attributed to any palaces or noble families dependent on the court in Potsdam, came from the homes of the upper classes.

If we speak of Frederician furniture in the narrower sense, then this term can only refer to those items that stood inside palaces or royal apartments and were made between 1740 and c. 1780. The main venues here are the palaces of Sanssouci, Charlottenburg, Potsdam, Breslau, and the New Palace, whose rooms Frederick the Great largely determined himself, even contributing his own drawings, as was reported by Anton Friedrich Büsching (1788) among others for the New Palace. This style only rarely crossed national borders. Some of the rooms in the residences of Zerbst Castle and Mirów Castle are evidence of the impact of Potsdam and Berlin designs of the mid-eighteenth century on neighbouring principalities. The furniture designed for Frederick the Great's palaces, be it

veneered ébéniste pieces or carved and painted sculptural items, are among the most important and consummate achievements of German furniture production in the eighteenth century. In many cases it can be seen as a perfect synthesis between a bright idea and brilliant craft implementation, as a communal work by those artists who shaped Frederician Rococo.

'There are highly outstanding artists of this kind here': Ébénistes and ornamental sculptors in and around the court at Potsdam

Nicolai's appraisal of the conditions in Potsdam in 1786 is hardly surprising, as there was an excellent market for luxury goods for a long time as a result of the royal commissions. Frederick almost exclusively used masters based in Potsdam or Berlin for the furniture of his palaces, as it had always been a concern of the rulers to support home-grown industry with demanding and well-paid commissions. These specialized artists and the member of their workshops, which worked on a division-of-labour principle, were often not born in Prussia, however. Instead they came in response to Frederick's summons, such as Melchior Kambly from Switzerland, the brothers Johann Friedrich and Heinrich Wilhelm Spindler from Bayreuth, and the brothers Johann Michael (the Elder) and Johann Christian (the Younger) Hoppenhaupt from Merseburg. The workshops themselves also employed craftsmen from other countries; it is known that Kambly employed French experts to work on bronze and tortoiseshell. Potsdam's cabinetmaker Johann Heinrich Hülsmann on the other hand was local. An excellent replica of Frederick the Great's French desk from Sanssouci Palace made by Hülsmann still survives, for example. Another example of a home-grown artist is Johann August Nahl, a sculptor from Berlin. They were all united by their commitment to a decorative style and furniture design whose fundamental direction was based on the tastes of Frederick the Great. This binding general principle often makes it difficult to attribute drawings of furniture designs, especially those by Nahl and the Hoppenhaupts. Friedrich Christian Glume and the architect Wenzeslaus von Knobelsdorff played an important role for the furniture of the early period of around 1740–45, even though there are only few examples by which their works and designs could be defined more closely. However, Knobelsdorff in particular can be called a pioneer and the one who set the path for Frederician furniture. The most important of these artists and artisans will be introduced in brief below.

First and foremost there is the sculptor Friedrich Christian Glume, who was already one of the pioneers of Frederician interior design from around 1737 onwards through his work in Rheinsberg and then also in Sanssouci Palace. However, his work in this regard is difficult to assess via the generally verifiable activity of making carved furniture. One of the pieces of furniture associated with him is the desk chair (probably still) from the late 1730s, which has a heavy feel and legs decorated with mascarons. Frederick the Great later had it turned into a wing-back armchair, using it as a desk chair in the bedroom and study of his apartment in the Potsdam City Palace throughout his life.

The style really started developing when Johann August Nahl was appointed. He was the son of a Berlin-based court sculptor who had worked under Schlüter, but left Prussia with his parents shortly after the death of Frederick I. In 1741 Nahl, after having received a well-grounded training in France, followed Frederick the Great's call, spending just six years as *directeur des ornements* in Berlin and Potsdam, significantly shaping the court's interior design of that time together with Knobelsdorff. One of the tasks of his workshop, in addition to producing the stucco decoration on the walls, was designing and making carved seating, tables and mirror frames for the palaces in Berlin and Potsdam. In 1746 he secretly and hastily left his employer, because he evidently no longer wanted to meet his overreaching job requirements and the burdens that resulted from the military moving into his home in Berlin. After stopping over in Switzerland, he went to the court of the landgrave of Hesse-Kassel in 1755, where he worked until his death in 1781.

The Hoppenhaupt brothers Johann Michael the Elder and Johann Christian the Younger followed Frederick the Great's call at the same time as Nahl. They came to Prussia from Merseburg in 1740, to first work under Knobelsdorff and Nahl, putting their interior designs into practice, and they also included carved furniture. They worked together on Sanssouci Palace (1746), for example in the concert room and bedroom, and they also created decorations and furniture for Frederick the Great's apartments in his palace in Berlin (1747) and in the Potsdam City Palace (1755, fig. 11). After Nahl's flight from Prussia, the younger Hoppenhaupt became his successor. During the 1760s he oversaw the works to decorate and furnish the New Palace. Johann Michael, who published a large number of his designs as engravings, returned to Merseburg in 1756, after he had completed, among other things, the extensive interior decoration and furnishing of von Bouman's new wing of (what is now) Wrocław Palace in 1752/53. In addition to Nahl and the Hoppenhaupts, who worked as designers and also makers of carved decorations and furniture, other sculptors are also listed in the sources as having produced furniture. Georg Franz Ebenhech for example, delivered silver-plated dining chairs for the Marschall dining room in Potsdam City Palace. Peter Schwitzer and Matthias Müller are documented as having produced console tables and mirror frames for the City Palace and Sanssouci.

The works by Kambly and the Spindler brothers enjoy special standing, as they had a hugely significant impact on the artistic and artisanal quality and the special position of Frederician furniture. The quality of the items produced by the sculptor Melchior Kambly, who had been resident in Potsdam since 1743 and who also produced carved and painted furniture and much more, lay mainly in his ability to make precious bronzes and furniture with a tortoiseshell veneer. Manger mentioned him for the first time as a supplier of 'armchairs and dining chairs' for Sanssouci Palace in 1746. In 1749 he copied, with some artistic input of his own, a document cabinet Frederick had purchased in Paris. He went on to repeat it as a more inexpensive version with gilded wood carvings for Breslau (Wrocław) Palace in 1752/53. He achieved fame, however, for his chests and tables covered lavishly with tortoiseshell, which he started producing for the City Palace in Potsdam in around 1755 and later also for the New Palace. Together with the equally popular fire-gilded and silver-plated bronzes, they stand for courtly furniture whose primary purpose was the presentation of material luxury in order to boost reputation.

The works by the brothers Johann Friedrich and Heinrich Wilhelm Spindler are among the top achievements of furniture manufacture in Potsdam during the second half of Frederick the Great's reign. The ébénistes from Bayreuth, who had been recruited in 1765 in connexion with the work on the New Palace's furnishings, brought Frederician furniture to a late climax with their marquetry techniques, which were remarkably diverse and executed with great skill. Both masters had their own separate workshops in Potsdam and in 1767 they both were awarded the rank of master. They mainly produced furniture, floors and panelling for the New Palace and in the 1770s also for the New Chambers in the marquetry technique typical of their workshops, which was usually characterized by floral decoration with framing ornamentation. There are some exceptional pieces of furniture among those produced by the younger Spindler, such as the *Papageien-Kommode* (Parrot Commode, probably 1769) and the *Drei-Grazien-Kommode* (Three Graces Commode, 1769), whose form and decoration are both unique

and at the same time characteristic of late Frederician Rococo furniture. These two pieces of furniture get their remarkable appeal from the combination of silver-plated bronzes (from the Kambly workshop) and opulent marquetry of tortoiseshell, mother-of-pearl, ivory and silver based on the Boulle technique (fig. 12). When royal commissions failed to materialize and the brothers started quarrelling, probably for that reason, Heinrich Wilhelm moved his work to Berlin in around 1779. Even before he moved he requested a licence to sell his furniture in other Prussian cities as well. After the lull in commissions, both workshops will have thereby increased their sales to the aristocracy and the wealthy citizenry, while probably adapting their style more to the fashion of giving furniture an antique look. However, after just over ten years of working for Frederick the Great, the golden age of their workshops was over in the mid-1770s.

'Tortoiseshell works', 'wood inlays' and 'gilded, sculpted ornament' – the style of the furniture for Frederick the Great's palaces

The guide books of the eighteenth century, which described the interiors of Potsdam's palaces to their readers, mainly chose to mention furniture because of their precious materials. Thus, the most commonly discussed pieces are those from the workshops of Melchior Kambly and the younger Spindler, which were adorned with tortoiseshell and metal inlays. The painted and gilded seating furniture and console tables by contrast were only mentioned very rarely. It was at most the console tables' preciously encrusted stone slabs that were named. However, it is particularly the carved furniture that makes the character of the room as an overall work of art especially vivid, as almost all of the pieces blend in smoothly and appropriately with the decorations that formed part of the walls.

The style of the carved furniture in the 1740s is illustrated by the seats in the Golden Gallery in Charlottenburg Palace or the seating furniture from Frederick's bedroom in the City Palace in Potsdam, which was based on Nahl's designs (fig. 10). They combine bold contours that seem almost exalted at times with highly skilful, incredibly vivid ornamentation: the lines of the legs and armrests swing backwards and forwards and their double s-shapes give them curving constructions, while the legs and backrest frames are covered in twining plants, while the open-worked shell ornaments in the frames give the furniture a springy lightness. Another object that probably falls into this phase of Frederician Rococo is a wall mirror whose stylistic characteristics, such as the wealth of ornamentation crowning the frame and the typical wing-feathers, can also be seen in Nahl's designs for the concert hall in Sanssouci and the bedroom in Potsdam's City Palace in the mid-1740s in a similar fashion (fig. 9). Nahl's vivid, imaginative style can also be found in the work of Johann Michael Hoppenhaupt the Elder, albeit in a somewhat robust fashion and more abstract in the details. One case in point is a folding screen from around 1745, now lost, that stood in the king's round study (designed by Nahl) in his Berlin Palace. This style then lives on in the carved seating furniture of the Hoppenhaupt brothers, which were produced around ten years later when the City Palace in Potsdam was refurnished. They are somewhat lacking in the vital, almost overflowing temperament of Nahl's works. Instead trends emerged that can also be seen in the later seating furniture produced for the New Palace in around 1765 under the auspices of the younger Hoppenhaupt: the tendency to larger, calmer shapes, the use of leg shapes tending towards the whimsical, and ornamentation that seems a little coarse at times. From time to time the seating furniture in the New Palace, made to the designs of the younger Hoppenhaupt, also demonstrate a turning towards the Neo-classical forms already well developed elsewhere without achieving the charm of some other objects from that transitional period. These works must be distinguished from the more delicate and subtle designs of the elder Hoppenhaupt, which he published as engravings in around 1753.

The shapes are particularly diverse in the large number of console and wall tables that we know of. Depending on their size they feature playful lightness as well as monumental heaviness. The ornamentation almost always has the most important role. It overrides the tectonic constraints of loads and support and makes these pieces look like a symphony of shells, vines, twining flowers, acanthus and abstract scaly ornaments.

The Frederician chests and cupboards evince a great spectrum of forms, which range from relatively simple inlaid pieces, or, more rarely, colourfully painted or gilded ones to items whose preciously inlaid surfaces are heightened through the use of lavish bronze ornaments and a veritable material excess. An inlaid cedar wood display cabinet in Charlottenburg Palace, based on a design by Knobelsdorff, is characteristic of the architectural design and finely balanced proportions of some of the pieces made in the 1740s. Next to this cabinet is a pair of markedly waisted commodes with their high legs and greatly narrowed waists from the king's residential rooms in Potsdam's City Palace, probably produced in Hülsmann's workshop. The near-exalted feel of the shapes used, and the finely balanced application of bronze ornaments are among the stylistic characteristics of Frederician furniture. Examples like this demonstrate just how far this style had distanced itself from its French models.

The best works from Kambly's and Heinrich Wilhelm Spindler's workshops during the period when the New Palace was being refurnished in around 1765/69 also demonstrate this detachment from the French rules of proportion and décor. It seems likely that almost all of their designs came from the younger Hoppenhaupt, but in the details the artisans definitely incorporated their own ideas. The commode with the parrot motif (fig. 12) in the study of Frederick's apartment, whose overlong dimension and lavish decor of floral and figurative motifs provide a magnificent spectacle, ignoring the restraint inherent in French Rococo furniture, is just one case in point. The reason for this could be that the younger Spindler was responsible for the commode as a whole, but the excellent bronzes came from Kambly's workshop. It is perceptible here and with other pieces of stately furniture that a kind of *paragone* took place between the two artists, a competition between the sculptural and the pictorial. This competition may not always have been to the advantage of the overall effect. It is entirely appropriate to assume that this ostentatious display of luxury goes back to a personal request by Frederick the Great, after all, the New Palace itself was basically pure display architecture.

JÖRG MEINER

Select Bibliography

Hintze 1930; Schreyer 1932; Bleibaum 1933; Huth 1958; Nicht 1980; Kreisel / Himmelheber 1983; Sangl 1991; Locker 2008; Schick 2008; Schöne 2009; Bergemann 2010; Graf 2011

Catalogue

Potsdam in the Eighteenth Century

If we are to accept Frederick the Great's assessment, Potsdam in his father's time was a 'wretched little place'. Most of the houses were not of stone, but timber-framed. But from 1744, the choice of Potsdam to be Frederick's principal place of residence went hand in hand with the remodelling of the City Palace and the building of Sanssouci. From 1748 the squares and other buildings of this small town on the Havel were also given an outward appearance worthy of a royal residence.

In 1740, the year of Frederick's accession, Potsdam was home to 11,700 civilians and 3,500 soldiers. Thanks to the king's deliberate policy of attracting new settlers and promoting economic activity, the population had risen by the time of his death in 1786 to 18,500 civilians and 6,500 military personnel. Thus even more markedly than under his father, the Soldier King, the military became a defining social and economic factor. There was one soldier to every three civilians, and under the billeting system, this soldier had to be provided with board and lodging. In spite of state subsidy programmes, the absence of the garrison in times of war led to severe economic crises. The Seven Years' War, especially, impoverished many of the city's inhabitants. IE

1

Report by the Potsdam Royal Guard

Potsdam 1783 | Paper, ink, 39 x 50 cm (open) | Berlin, GStA PK, I. HA,
Rep. 96, no. 412 C2, sheet 33−34v | Literature: Voltaire 1784

As we know from Voltaire's memoirs, Frederick the Great
required himself to be informed every day about who was
visiting Potsdam. In the Secret State Archive one such *Report
by the Potsdam Royal Guard* dating from the later part of
Frederick's reign has survived. On 6 September 1783 it was
recorded who entered and left through the five gates of the city.
In addition to the occupation, home, and destination of the trav-
eller, the reasons for the journey were usually also documented.
This source thus makes it possible to say something about the
number of people visting Potsdam on a given day, their social
background, and their reason for travelling. Four groups of visitors and their motivations can be distinguished. Firstly, members of the garrison and the court were moving about the city.
Secondly, numerous private individuals had petitions to present
to the king, and they passed through Potsdam on their way to
Sanssouci: envoys, students, military invalids, colonists, manufacturers, craftsmen, farmers, court gardeners, and shep-
herds. The third group comprised tradesmen and merchants
who had goods to sell in the city. At the end of the source, as
a fourth group, four barges from Hamburg are listed, laden with
luxury items such as coffee, tobacco, wine, sugar and syrup,
as well as raw materials for the factories such as saltpetre, tur-
pentine and cotton. It is striking that Potsdam was primarily
the destination of visitors from Berlin. With 15 recorded in-
gresses and 16 egresses, the Berlin Gate was the most-fre-
quented entry and exit. IE

2

Postmaster General Gustav Adolph, Count von Gotter (1692−1762) Playing the Bagpipes

Antoine Pesne (Paris 1683−1757 Berlin) | Berlin, c. 1730 | Oil on can-
vas, 106 x 86.5 x 8 cm | Bayreuth, BSV, Neues Schloss, purchased with
the support of the Ernst von Siemens Kunststiftung, inv. no. Bay NS.
G 123 and Ernst von Siemens Kunstfond, inv. no. Bay NS. L-G 28 |
Literature: Börsch-Supan 1986; Zick 1992, esp. pp. 91−96; exhib. cat.
Paradies des Rokoko 1998, vol. 2, p. 182, cat. no. 182; Krückmann
2001, p. 244

Gustav Adolph, Count von Gotter, was born in Gotha and had
an impressive career. In 1724 he became an imperial baron,
and in 1740 Frederick II made him an imperial count, appointing him *Oberhofmarschall* (head of the court administration)
and privy councillor. Throughout his life he stood in the king's
favour; he was also appointed Director General of the Berlin

Opera, and finally, Postmaster General. Gotter was responsible
for the first express postal services in Prussia; they were established between Potsdam and Berlin in 1754. He seems to have
been not only successful, but also extremely diplomatic and
agreeable. His company was valued by Prince Eugen in Vienna
no less than it was by Frederick in Prussia. Another sign of the
latter's particular appreciation is the fact that no less an artist
than the Parisian-born court painter Antoine Pesne was commissioned to paint him, not once, but a number of times. The
Stiftung Preussische Schlösser und Gärten Berlin-Brandenburg
owns a portrait of Gotter and his niece Friederike von Wangen-
heim in pilgrim's garb, painted in 1750, while the present portrait, dating from some twenty years earlier, shows the sitter
as a man nearing forty. Pesne places Gustav Adolph Count von
Gotter in profile as regards the body, but with his head facing
the beholder. He is wearing a red velvet jacket, a white cravat,
a bluish-green coat, and a beret with a feather. In costume and
depicted playing the bagpipes, he is transferred to the world of
Antoine Watteau and his bucolic *fêtes galantes*. Gotter's Thur-

Potsdam in the Eighteenth Century

ingian seat, Schloss Molsdorf, was decorated by the stucco worker Giovanni Antonio Pedrozzi, who was also patronized by Frederick and his sister Wilhelme of Bayreuth. JG

3–4

Design for a city gate, perhaps the Brandenburg Gate in Potsdam

Probably Carl von Gontard (Mannheim 1731–1791 Breslau, now Wrocław) | Berlin or Potsdam, last third of 18th c. | Ink wash drawing, with pencil, 22.6 x 29.3 cm (sheet), 42 x 56 x 3.5 cm (overall) | Potsdam, SPSG, Plankammer, inv. no. PK 5352

Design for the Neustadt Gate in Potsdam

Georg Wenzeslaus von Knobelsdorff (Kuckädel bei Crossen, now Kukadło 1699–1753 Berlin) | Berlin or Potsdam 1753 | Ink drawing with pencil, 22.1 x 36.6 cm (sheet), 42 x 56 x 3.5 cm (overall) | Potsdam, SPSG, Plankammer, inv. no. PK 4215

Literature: Giersberg 1986; exhib. cat. Knobelsdorff 1999, pp. 257–259

As part of the beautification measures, in 1753 the western end of Breite Strasse, with the Neustadt Gate, also became the subject of attention. The latter structure was not exactly a noble sight, and as far as traffic to and from Potsdam was concerned, it was of no great importance. The king himself, when going to Sanssouci, normally used the more northerly Brandenburg Gate. Knobelsdorff, who in 1748 gave the Breite Strasse a gate-like entry in the form of numbers 13 and 14 Schlossstrasse, was now commissioned to round off this important boulevard in worthy style in the form of a newly designed Neustadt Gate.

He designed a Classical ensemble with a customs and guard house, along with a centrally opening wrought-iron gate for the central passage. The side facing the city was given loggias left and right, each formed of three round arches. On their attic storeys were placed castellations which underscored the fortress-like character. Behind, and standing back a little, were the rooms for the guards and the customs officers. The one-sided character of the gate, oriented entirely towards the Breite Strasse, became even more apparent when looking at the side facing away from the city. Here the buildings were plain, with low skillion roofs. The design climax of the gate was a pair of obelisks, standing on high plinths, and surmounted by eagle weather-vanes. The elaborate but meaningless pseudo-hiero-glyphs on the sides reveal the period's great interest in the exotic and cryptic, and were, together with the typical form of the obelisks, interpreted as symbols of power. In 1945 the Neustadt Gate was destroyed. The south obelisk was rescued, however, and in 1981, after its restoration, it was re-erected not far from its original location, albeit without the eagle. TS

4
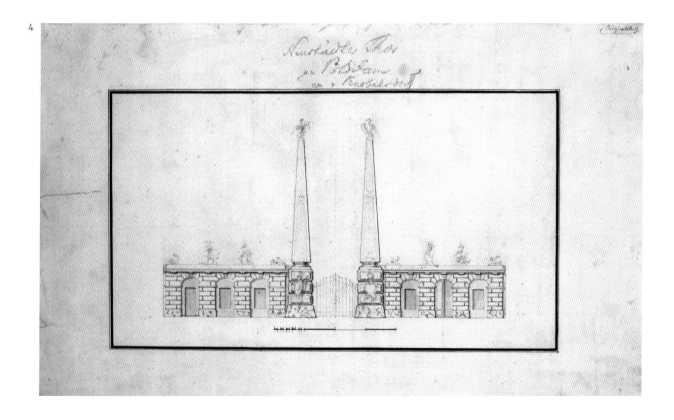

The Hunters' Gate (Jägertor) in Potsdam

Dismar Degen (Holland c. 1700–1753 Potsdam) | Potsdam c. 1735 |
Oil on canvas, 67 x 103 cm | Potsdam, SPSG, inv. no. GK I 9280 | Literature: Nicolai 1786

The *Jägertor* or Hunters' Gate, dating from 1733, is, alongside the Brandenburg Gate and the Nauen Gate, one of the three surviving city gates of Potsdam. It was built as part of the Baroque enlargement of the city under the Prussian king Frederick William I, and is the oldest of the gates still to retain its original form. Situated between Lindenstrasse and Jägerallee, the gate, formerly embedded in the city wall (*Akzisemauer*), bounded the city to the north. It served to prevent customs evasion and desertion by soldiers. The city wall and the gate buildings having been demolished in the nineteenth century, the Hunters' Gate now stands as an isolated structure.

The Dutch artist Dismar Degen shows the gate, whose size he exaggerates, in the midst of everyday hustle and bustle: the portals are open, the city and the gate itself are under military guard. While huntsmen are riding to hounds, goods are being delivered and people are being driven into the city in carriages. The painting, which dates from just two years after the erection of the gate, was probably commissioned by the king to bear witness to his achievements as a patron of architecture. In around 1730, Dismar Degen was active in Prussia as court painter to Frederick William I. Apart from city views, he also painted battle scenes and landscapes. Although Friedrich Nicolai described him in 1786 as a 'mediocre painter of prospects and battles', the painting itself was highly thought of. In the eighteenth century it was hung in the royal dining room in the Potsdam City Palace. AB

6

Frederick II of Prussia

Studio of Antoine Pesne (Paris 1683–1757 Berlin) | Berlin c. 1750 |
Oil on canvas, 75 x 55.6 cm | Potsdam, Potsdam Museum, inv. no.
V 81/1246 K | Literature: Hildebrand 1942

The portrait of the young king was executed in the studio of the court painter Antoine Pesne. Frederick appears here in the

5

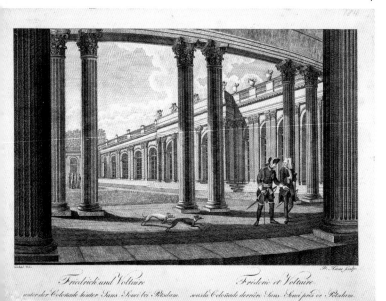

Friedrich und Voltaire   Frédéric et Voltaire
unter der Colonade hinter Sans Souci bei Potsdam.   sous la Colonade derrière Sans Souci près de Potsdam.

Secret News of Voltaire's Life, written by himself

François Marie Arouet, alias Voltaire (Paris 1694–1778 Paris) | Berlin 1784 | Book, 18.3 x 23.7 x 2 cm | Berlin, SBB PK, inv. no. As 15005

Literature: Bisky 2011; Pleschinski 2011

François-Marie Arouet, known as Voltaire, was already France's most influential universal genius, freethinker, writer and journalist, when Frederick entered into correspondence with him in 1736. The philosopher was flattered by the gushing words of the crown prince when at home he had been the subject of censorship and threats of arrest by the court in Versailles and the *parlement de Paris*; Frederick was impressed by Voltaire's way of life and way of thinking, and not least by his European renown. Thus began a turbulent relationship: Frederick's youthfully fresh opinions, which at first Voltaire found very promising, came to an end in the first years of his rule and the wars that accompanied it. 'Without heroism and the throne, you would have become the most lovable man in society,' Voltaire wrote with some bitterness.

Soon afterwards, Voltaire visited the Prussian court a number of times, but only ever briefly, also between June and November 1743, and was unmasked as a spy of the French king. Even so, he and Frederick maintained their correspondence, exchanging views on philosophy, science and literature, with mutual flattery and criticism. As Voltaire found no lasting recognition in Versailles, after the death of his lover, the cultured Marquise du Châtelet (1706–1749), he accepted Frederick's invitation to come to Potsdam. The philosophers' paradise! That was how the king wanted his Sanssouci to be seen. Voltaire stayed from 1750 to 1753. Then his feuds and business dealings, and not least his doubts about the king's friendly intentions, led to a breach with the Prussian court. Frederick snarled: 'Until you came, there was peace in my house.'

In spite of everything, the two men resumed their correspondence. When Voltaire died in 1778, the Prussian ruler gave a eulogy in the Berlin Academy. He even had mass said for the lifelong anticlericalist in St Hedwig's cathedral in Berlin. The love-hate relationship of the two was already interpreted in different ways by contemporaries. Each profited from the influence and renown of the other, so that the boundary lines between self-interest and genuine sympathy were difficult to draw. Ultimately both were similarly self-centred, artists, if you will, who with their correspondence, their gestures of friendship and their discord still captivate us today. MD

gala uniform of the chief of the 1st Guard Battalion, in other words his personal bodyguard. This uniform is identical to that worn by him in the portrait by Fischer senior. However, the hats are different: on the present picture, it is still the small one: it became increasingly voluminous from the mid-1750s. Fischer's portrait, by contrast, shows one of the larger variants, but still with silver embroidery. By the end of the Seven Years' War, finally, this had become the characteristically Frederician upright tricorne without embroidery, but with a bow and white ostrich plumes. There exists a letter from the king to his valet Fredersdorff dated 8 August 1748 concerning the making of two uniform jackets for 500 reichstaler each. It is altogether possible that the two pictures both show the gala uniform described in the letter, made of dark-blue velvet with a silver-embroidered waistcoat. This, and the coronation robe below left, would then be a terminus post quem for a dating of the picture. In general it is not easy to date most of the royal portraits painted between 1740 and 1763, as Frederick refused, after 1740, to sit for his portraits, which were mostly from then on based on the famous likeness of him as crown prince by Pesne, painted in 1739. TS

7–8

Frederick and Voltaire

Christian Peter Jonas Haas (Copenhagen 1754–1804 Berlin) | Probably Berlin c. 1790 | Etching, 17.5 x 26.8 cm | Potsdam, Potsdam Museum, inv. no. V 80/151 K2a

Royal Construction Projects in Potsdam

Potsdam owes its reputation as a small but all the more select showpiece of European architecture and city planning to one man alone: Frederick II of Prussia, known as 'the Great'. During the 46 years of his reign, he turned the 'wretched little place' (as he himself described the city as it had been in his father's day), into a royal residence with paved streets and squares, which were almost without exception lined by splendid buildings. The king had more than 600 new houses built for the citizenry. For the Scottish physician John Moore, Potsdam had 'every requisite to form an agreeable town, if by that word is meant the streets, stone walls, and external appearance. But if a more complex idea be annexed to the word, and if it be thought to comprehend the finishing, furniture, and conveniences within the houses, in that case Potsdam is a very poor town indeed.' Moore recognized, like other contemporaries, the stage-set character of the royal residence on the Havel, which, with its copies of English, French and Italian palaces, seemed to have sprung from the maxim of Marc-Antoine Laugier, who thought: 'If you want a nicely built city, you must on no account leave the design of the façades of the private houses to the whims of their owners.' TS

Nauensche Plantage from the North

Andreas Ludwig Krüger (Potsdam 1743–1822 Berlin) after a painting
by Johann Friedrich Meyer | Potsdam after 1773 | Inscribed: La rüe
de Nauen et celle de tous les Environs tels qu'ils se représentent aux
venans du Nord | Pencil, Indian ink, wash, 63.8 x 84.6 cm (sheet),
51 x 73.8 cm (image) | Berlin, SMB PK, Kupferstichkabinett, inv. no.
D/K 126

The Roman Customs House on the Piazza di Pietra

Giovanni Battista Piranesi (Mogliano Veneto/Treviso 1720–1778 Rome) |
Rome 1753 | Inscribed: Veduta della Dogana di Terra a Piazza di Pietra |
Etching, 53.8 x 77.3 cm (sheet), 44.5 x 59.9 cm (plate) | Potsdam,
Potsdam Museum, inv. no. V 81/1362 K2/8

Literature: Manger 1789/90; Fick 2000, p. 89f.

One of the first commissions of the architect Carl von Gontard, who had come to Potsdam from Bayreuth in 1764, was
to renew the Nauensche Plantage, today's Platz der Einheit.
On three pages, he designed monumental façades behind
each of which, as a rule, two houses were concealed. In addition to the complex on the north side, which was based in
1767 on a design for a city hall in Paris that was never carried out, and whose uniform façade conceals a total of six

houses, the columned house built a year later was doubtless
the most striking building in the square. In the middle of the
otherwise rather bland façades, what was built here 'based
on a sketch by the king' was an architecture of dramatic
effects, which was mainly intended as the *point de vue* of a
visual axis starting at the Nauen Gate. This great façade too
concealed two individual houses.

The model was the Dogana di Terra, the papal customs
house in Rome, which was erected for Pope Innocent XII in
1695 by Francesco Fontana, directly behind the columns of
the north side of the Temple of Hadrian dating from 145 AD.
The latter's 'ruin' character was preserved in the process,
and lent the whole ensemble a decidedly picturesque quality. Gontard, who had personally seen the Dogana, added a
column for Potsdam, but did without the 'ruinous' appearance of the Roman model. The columned house was destroyed in 1945 and its completely preserved façade demolished in 1958. TS

Sketches for the houses Schwertfegergasse 1

Frederick II (Berlin 1712–1786 Potsdam) | c. 1753 | Indian ink on pa-
per, 25.5 x 21.7 cm (sheet) | Eichenzell, HH, Archiv Schloss Fasanerie,
Autographen-Sammlung KF 1.2-5/a

9

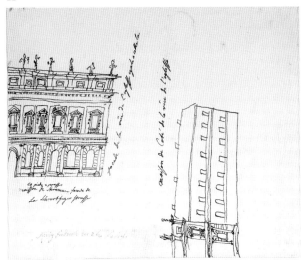

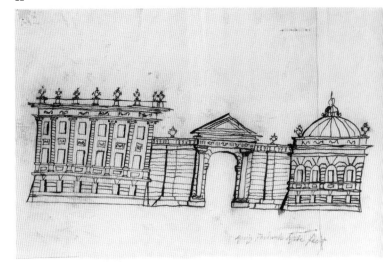

Sketch for the house Am Kanal 3

Frederick II | 1751/52 | Indian ink on paper, 18.8 x 37 cm (sheet) | Eichen-
zell, HH, Archiv Schloss Fasanerie, Autographen-Sammlung KF 1.2-5/b

Sketch for 'the last two houses in the Breite Strasse'

Frederick II | c. 1753 | Indian ink on paper, 21 x 25.5 cm (sheet) | Eichen-
zell, HH, Archiv Schloss Fasanerie, Autographen-Sammlung KF 1.2-5/c

Literature: Manger 1789/90; Mielke 1972; Giersberg 1986; Mielke 1981

Until about ten years before his death, Frederick II sometimes took a very intense interest in architecture in all its contemporary and historical variations. He did not content himself with observing it either in situ or in drawings and paintings, but also tried his hand at it himself. Of hundreds of sketches, though, just two dozen survive. They make two things clear. On the one hand, the king, unlike his great-great-nephew Frederick William IV, was quite certainly no great draughtsman, whether with or without ruler and compasses. As Frederick's view of architecture was decidedly 'external', aiming for effect, he did not think through the constructional or functional implications of his designs, but only their decorative aspects. In most of the sketches, he relied heavily on Palladio, Vitruvius and other recognized role models, and in the process, like a child, adopted their architectural designs if anything instinctively. On the other hand, though, it is surprising how concretely these façades were executed in fact. For all their amateurism, they were never thought of as ends in themselves or as a playful search for a personal architectural expression, but, as Tilo Eggeling put it, as 'drawn Cabinet orders'. The precise indications of location, of the length and height of the façades, of the column orders to be used, and of the future occupants, make it clear that Frederick, unlike his great-great-nephew, was concerned not with fantasies but with concrete building projects. The present hand drawings were all implemented more or less as depicted. The house Am Kanal 3, built in 1752, intended for the commander of the Garde du Corps, the king's mounted bodyguard, still stands. TS

View of Potsdam and Sanssouci (seen from Eiche)

Georg Wenzeslaus von Knobelsdorff (Kuckädel bei Crossen [now Kukadło
near Krosno Odrzańskie] 1699 – 1753 Berlin) | 1750 | Oil on canvas,
88.1 x 119.5 cm | Potsdam, SPSG, inv. no. GK I 5692 | Literature:
Oesterreich 1773, p. 68, no. 331; Nicolai 1786, p. 1216; Staatliche
Schlösser 1990, pp. 82, 83, 147, no. 108; exhib. cat. Friedrich II. und
die Kunst 1986, p. 175, no. XIV.4; exhib. cat. Knobelsdorff 1999, cat.
no. I.8, pp. 174 – 176 with ill.

Like a bright vision on the horizon, we see Sanssouci Palace, the ruins on the Höneberg, and the skyline of Potsdam in the midst of the Havel landscape of Brandenburg. Dating from 1750, the atmospheric depiction by Knobelsdorff shows two of the most important architectural and landscape changes in Potsdam to be implemented by Frederick in the early years of his reign: Sanssouci and the follies and reservoir on the Höneberg, the latter intended to supply the planned water features in the park. These had been completed three and two years earlier, respectively. At the same time, in this painting the court artist Knobelsdorff emphasizes his own achievements: a versatile figure, he was both a painter and an architect, the superintendent of the royal buildings, and, albeit briefly, director of drama and music. At the age of thirty, he ended his service in the army, and devoted himself to painting. During this period he came into contact with Frederick, then crown prince. Although he only took up architecture later, he set the tone in this field. His painting was largely devoted to portraits and landscapes. In contrast to what one might expect, however, in this *View of Potsdam and Sanssouci* the focus is not on the exact reproduction of the architecture, but rather on a picturesque and atmospheric depiction. The picture has been on display in Sanssouci since 1773. AB

15

Alter Markt with Old City Hall, St Nicholas's Church and City Palace (Fig. 1, p. 8/9)

Carl Christian Wilhelm Baron (1737–1775) | Potsdam 1772 | Oil on canvas, 84.5 x 125.5 cm | Potsdam, SPSG, inv. no. GK I 15748 | Literature: Oesterreich 1773, p. 55; Oesterreich 1775, pp. 10–11; Eckhardt/ Giersberg/Bartoschek 1996, pp. 114–119; Becker 2005, pp. 222–223

Immediately after the completion of the Alter Markt in the 1770s, vedutas were already being painted, for example by Johann Friedrich Meyer and Carl Christian Wilhelm Baron. The king had these views hung in the guest apartments in the New

Chambers in Sanssouci. They include the artistic version of the Frederician design for the square, painted by Carl Christian Wilhelm Baron in 1772.

The description by Matthias Oesterreich, inspector of the royal picture gallery, reveals the king's unqualified praise: 'Prospect of the Alter Markt in Potsdam, with the City Church, the City Hall and a part of the Royal Palace; very nice, diligently painted on canvas, by the painter Baron in Potsdam. The reality is excellently imitated with a good effect, and does great honour to this skilful artist among connoisseurs. […] The painting has been highly praised by His Majesty the King.'.

The veduta directs the gaze of the beholder across the busy square, which is characterized by market stalls and artistic performances, to the northern side, with St Nicholas's Church in the middle. Slightly obscured by the obelisks in the square, we can see the Roman-inspired façade porch constructed under Frederick. It was completed in 1755 as a smaller copy of the façade of S. Maria Maggiore built twelve years earlier to plans by Ferdinando Fuga. In the left foreground is the adjoining west side of the Alter Markt with the cropped theatre wing of the City Palace, and on the right the lively eastern side of the

14

square with the Old City Hall. Between this and the church we can see, foreshortened, the front of the parish schoolhouse and presbytery. JG

16–17

The Alter Markt in Potsdam

Johann Friedrich Schleuen (1739–1784) | Potsdam c. 1770 | Inscribed: Prospect des alten Marckts zu Potsdam [...] | Etching, 32 x 48 cm (sheet), 29.1 x 41.6 cm (plate) | Potsdam, Potsdam Museum, inv. no. V 79/93 K2a

View of the Basilica di Santa Maria Maggiore with the two buildings to the side (Fig. 4, p. 14)

Giovanni Battista Piranesi (Mogliano Veneto/Treviso 1720–1778 Rome) | c. 1746/48 | Inscribed: Veduta della Basilica di Santa Maria Maggiore con le due Fabbriche laterali di detta Basilica; bottom right: Piranesi del Scol. | Etching, 53.8 x 77.3 cm (sheet), 40 x 55 cm (plate) | Berlin, SMB PK, Kupferstichkabinett, inv. no. AM 63-1955

Literature: Drescher/Kroll 1981, p. 46, cat. no. 112; Robinson 1983, pp. 18–21; exhib. cat. La Roma di Piranesi 2006, p. 137; exhib. cat. Vedute di Roma 2007, p. 57, cat. no. 9; Sölter 2007, esp. pp. 16–17

For the layout of what is now the Alter Markt, Frederick II undertook an intensive study of European architecture and architectural theory. On the north side of the Alter Markt stood St Nicholas's church, a cruciform structure built during the reign of his father Frederick William I. Between 1752 and 1755, Frederick had a new façade built in the style of the Roman High Baroque for the southern arm of the cross, which gave on to the square. The view of the Alter Markt etched by Johann Friedrich Schleuen, which also served as a model used for a sheet in the raree show operated by Johann Christoph Nabholz, shows the two-storey façade, which is elaborately structured by columns and pilasters, surmounted by round and triangular pediments.

The king based his design for the new façade on the work of the Italian architects Sanmicheli and Ferdinando Fuga, which he knew from prints by Piranesi. Specifically, he demanded an adaptation of the façade of S. Maria Maggiore in Rome, which Fuga had built twelve years earlier.

The architect, artist and archaeologist Giovanni Battista Piranesi, born in Venice in 1720, had become very well known above all through his series Vedute di Roma. Immediately after his arrival in Rome in 1740, he undertook an intensive study of Roman architecture, and in 1748 he created the first etchings in a series that eventually ran to a total of 137 works. He depicted the basilica of S. Maria Maggiore in a slightly oblique view, placing it in the centre ground of the picture. The view from below makes the building look even more monumental. The squares in Potsdam and Rome are comparable not only by dint of the architectural analogies, but also of the obelisk and column, respectively, in the centre of each. Like Piranesi, Schleuen also enlivens his vedute with the inclusion of people and props in the foreground. JG

18

Memorial Plaque to Major General Friedrich Wilhelm von Rohdich

Anonymous artist | 1790 | Inscribed: Friderich Wilhelm von Rohdich/ Den Helden ein Muster/Den Bürgern ein Trost/Den Armen ein Vater/ Drei Königen Werth./Vom Magistrat und der Bürgerschaft/aus Dankbar-keit errichtet anno 1790. [Friedrich Wilhelm von Rohdich/a model for heroes/a comfort for citizens/a father to the poor/of service to three kings/The council and citizenry/erected this in gratitude anno 1790] | Spruce, pine, beech, lime, painted in various colours, plaster medallion 175 x 70 x 15 cm | Potsdam, Potsdam Museum, inv. no. P 79/175

Friedrich Wilhelm (von) Rohdich was Prussia's first Minister of War under Frederick William II. Born in 1719 as the son of a sergeant-major in Potsdam, Rohdich attended the Joachims-thalsches Gymnasium (high school) and embarked on a career in the Royal Guards. For his various services in the Seven Years' War, he was awarded the medal 'Pour le Mérite' on a number of occasions and ennobled by Frederick the Great. After further promotions, Frederick appointed him commander of the Guards regiment in Potsdam and General Inspector of the Infantry in 1776. Finally in 1779 he became head of the Guards regiment, Potsdam City Commandant, and at the same time co-overseer of the Grand Military Orphanage.

Probably his most important measure during his time in Potsdam was to reform the billeting system after the death of Frederick. Since the time of Frederick's father Frederick William I, every citizen of Potsdam had been obliged to provide board and lodging in his house for up to six soldiers. Rohdich drew up a decree to 'regulate future arrangements between the local garrison and the citizens on whom the soldiers are billeted'. This measure substantially reduced the financial and other burdens on the citizenry resulting from the billeting process. In 1790 the citizenry in turn thanked their (by now former) City Commandant by presenting him, in his lifetime, with an elaborately designed memorial plaque with his image. By then, von Rohdich was already living in Berlin, as Frederick William II had appointed him, in 1787, to the post of Minister of State and War. Until the start of the twentieth century the memorial plaque hung in Potsdam City Hall. RS

19

Inn sign 'Zum Einsiedler' ('The Hermit')

Johann Peter Benckert (Bad Neuhaus 1709–1765 Potsdam) | Potsdam c. 1760 | Limewood, painted, 200 x 180 x 30 cm | Potsdam, Potsdam Museum, inv. no. P 80/289 | Literature: Mielke 1972; Volk 1988

In his biography of Alexander the Great, the Greek scholar and philosopher Plutarch related an anecdote concerning his compatriot Diogenes of Sinope. According to this story, Alexander visited the philosopher and offered to grant him a wish, whereupon the latter said: 'Please move a little out of the sun.' The king is said to have sighed, later: 'If I were not Alexander, I would like to be Diogenes.'

The Franconian sculptor Johann Peter Benckert transferred this anecdote to a relief and used it as a sign for the inn 'Zum Einsiedler' ('The Hermit'), which he had acquired in 1760. The house had in fact been named after its former owner, Count von Einsiedel; until its destruction in 1945 it stood between Hohewegstrasse and Schlossstrasse, right opposite the City Palace.

What did Benckert want to say with this relief? Diogenes sitting in his barrel is doubtless an allusion to the name of the

19

inn. To his right, two putti are playing with a wine bottle and a goblet as symbols of leisure. Alexander is laying his left arm on the barrel and looking down at the philosopher. To his left a leopard is leaping with bared teeth, a symbol of power and strength. Above the barrel we see the Prussian eagle, which (in line with the royal motto *Nec soli cedit*) famously yields not even to the sun, and takes both Diogenes and the king under his wing. The relief, which dates from the time of the Seven Years' War, contrasts two contradictory maxims. On the one hand, we see the king, who sees himself as the first servant of his state and whose ambition and thirst for glory would allow Prussia and Europe no peace: a sovereign of power. That at the same time he should set himself up as the philosopher of Sanssouci, and hence on the same level as Diogenes, is not without a certain irony. And on the other stands the philosopher, free of expectations and desires, devoting his life to his natural requirements, knowledge, and the joy of living: a sovereign of the spirit. Diogenes unambiguously occupies the centre ground, Alexander stands to one side: it is obvious which of them Benckert sympathized with. This inn sign is an example of bourgeois confidence in the face of feudal power, unusual for the time, and yet highly visible.

The finely worked relief is in a seriously degraded condition today. The cause is probably a fire in the nineteenth century, after which the losses were reconstructed and the whole surface painted over in the colour of the façade. During the 1980s, all these additions were removed and the artwork restored to its original state. TS/OMW

20–21 a-d
Head of a nature spirit: Fragment of the Apollo group
Johann Peter Benckert (Bad Neuhaus 1709–1765 Potsdam) | Sandstone, 36 cm (total height), 12 cm (height of base) | Berlin, SPSG, Skulpturensammlung, inv. no. 3897

Four drawings of statues and groups of statues: The Air, after Lambert Sigisbert Adam
Johann Peter Benckert | India ink, black, 38.4 x 25 cm | Inscribed l.: Adam fecit; r.: Joañ Peter Benckert gezeichnet 1763 27. Meÿen | Potsdam, Potsdam Museum, inv. no. V 81/123 K3

Apollo and three nature spirits: View from left
Johann Peter Benckert | India ink, black, pen, 35 x 25 cm | Inscribed r.: Joann Peter Benckert inV. et fecit 1763.20. a. gezeichnet nach dem Modell | Potsdam, Potsdam Museum, inv. no. 81/124 K3

Bearded old man, holding a torch to the chest of a young man
Johann Peter Benckert | India ink, black, pen, wash, 38 x 25 cm | Potsdam, Potsdam Museum, inv. no. V 81/125 K3

Venus
Johann Peter Benckert | India ink, black, pen, wash, 38.4 x 25.3 cm | Inscribed l.: PicGalle fcit; r.: Joann Peter Benckert gez. 1763 13. Junÿ | Potsdam, Potsdam Museum, inv. no. V 81/122 K3

Literature: Exhib. cat. Königliche Visionen 2003, pp. 214f. (with ill.); Götzmann 2009, pp. 55–56, cat. no. I.36–I.38

From several indications, quite apart from the number of commissions, it is clear that Johann Peter Benckert was greatly appreciated by the king. One is the decision to replace the sandstone statues of Apollo and Hercules by Georg Franz Ebenhech, which had been erected at the entrance to the central risalit on the courtyard side of the City Palace in Potsdam only in 1746, with the two groups centring on Apollo and Minerva, each accompanied by three nature spirits. The unusual charm of these works, which were destroyed in 1945, and their graceful, playful wealth of detail, can only be appreciated today from

21d

photographs and two fragments of heads. They were first recorded on paper by Benckert himself: eleven India ink drawings by him of masterpieces such as the allegory of *The Air*
by Lambert Sigisbert Adam, and the Venus by Jean-Baptiste
Pigalle from Sanssouci Park, but also of several of his own
works, such as the never-executed Prometheus giving the
breath of life to a youth, are preserved in the Potsdam Museum.
The uniform appearance of the rare sheets, with their black
edge, the clear lineation and the careful attribution of the
authorship both of the sculptures and the drawings, suggests
that they were intended for sale, or for an edition of copper
engravings. That this would have been inconceivable without
the king's assent is a further indication of the royal favour.

Also unusual is the stone epitaph in the form of a splendid
funerary sculpture, although it cannot be proved, as it has been
for Johann Joachim Quantz, that the commission came from
the king. While it is still usually attributed to Benckert himself,
this is by no means certain. The impressive likeness speaks
against this being a workshop piece, but on the other hand, the
advanced silicosis, which must have weakened the sculptor for
a long time, is a reason for thinking it cannot be by him. SH

22

Portrait bust of Margrave Frederick of Bayreuth

Giovanni Battista Pedrozzi (Pazzalino/Lugano 1710–1778 or 1779 Paz-
zalino/Lugano) | Bayreuth c. 1760 | Plaster and wood; 90 x 48 x 45 cm
(bust), 126 x 56 x 56 cm (base) | Bayreuth, BSV, Neues Schloss, inv.
no. BayNS. P0005 | Literature: Weber-Kellermann 1990, pp. 246–249
and p. 15; Endres 1998; exhib. cat. Paradies des Rokoko 1998, vol. 2,
p. 143, cat. no. 19 and p. 142, cat. no. 18, also unpublished material in
the museum

Frederick William I of Prussia was concerned to extend his
sphere of influence in southern Germany too, and concentrated
in particular on the important principalities of Ansbach and
Bayreuth, which were ruled by members of the house of Hohenzollern. To this end, he employed a strategic matrimonial
policy. In her memoirs, Frederick II's sister Wilhelmine writes
how she was pressured by their father, and how as a result of
her marriage to the young Margrave Frederick of Bayreuth, she
brought about a reconciliation between the Soldier King and
his son (later Frederick II). The latter maintained close contact
with his sister, which doubtless formed the basis of the em-
ployment of important Bayreuth court artists in Potsdam from
1763 on. Among them from 1764 was the Italian plaster artist
and sculptor Giovanni Battista Pedrozzi.

Pedrozzi's bust shows Margrave Frederick of Bayreuth,
who ruled from 1735 to 1763, as a no longer young man. The
portrait is cropped down to the helmeted head and a hint of the
shoulders. Unlike an almost contemporaneous bust by the
same sculptor, it depicts the sitter not in a contemporary breast-
plate, but in pseudo-Antique garments. The cloth is draped
loosely around the shoulders, which are decorated with a lion's
head and a lion's paw, attributes of Hercules. The helmet is or-
namented with ostrich plumes and a dragon. In spite of the
pseudo-classical paraphernalia, the eighteenth century still
shows through unmistakably in the wig and in the neckcloth,
which resembles the jabot of the Rococo period. JG

Luxury and Utilitarian Goods from Potsdam Factories

Under Frederick II, Potsdam factories profited more strongly from state support policies than did Berlin-based enterprises. The city where the king resided was to impress visitors not just with its buildings, parks and works of art, but also with its economic activity.

Originally Potsdam had neither a strong merchant presence nor competitive factories. Furthermore, there was no well-heeled citizenry with money to spend. The most important economic factors were the court and the garrison. Not surprisingly, therefore, the eighteenth century in Potsdam witnessed the growth in production particularly of luxury goods and military requisites. Frederick II hastened this process by bringing in new labour, providing credit for businessmen, building factories, and granting monopolies, especially in the textile sector. At the same time, imports of rival products were banned. This state support programme was a blessing and a curse at the same time. For while on the one hand it reduced the impact of the economic crisis resulting from the Seven Years' War, Potsdam manufacturers, artists and merchants were dependent on the king for orders, commissions and subsidies. IE

Three fragments of painted silk 'Peking' wallpaper from the New Palace

Isaac Joël factory | Glienicke hunting lodge (near Potsdam) c. 1768 | Silk, painted, 20 x 60 cm | Potsdam, SPSG, inv. no. IX 5530 D 77

Lease for Glienicke hunting lodge (near Potsdam) for Isaac Joël

Berlin 1764 | Paper, ink, embossed seal, 37 x 45 cm | Fulda, HH, Archiv Schloss Fasanerie, autograph collection KF 1.2-5/i

Instruction by Count Tauentzien regarding the issue of a deed gifting Glienicke hunting lodge to Isaac Joël

Breslau (Wrocław) 1759 | Paper, ink, 36 x 44 cm | Potsdam, BLHA, Rep. 19, Steuerrat Potsdam, no. 3004, sheet 9, 9v

Literature: Markgraf 1894; Stengel 1958; Herzfeld 1993; exhib. cat. Textile Kostbarkeiten 1993, p. 80, cat. no. 58; Beckert 2008; Evers/Zitzmann, currently being printed, cat. no. 19

The three fragments lying loosely on museum board covered in silk taffeta were recovered from a bedroom in the apartment of the Marquis d'Argens in the New Palace in 1970, along with other fragments, as remains of the original wall hangings dating from 1767. The pattern can be recognized on larger pieces which are not in a state to be exhibited (fig. 5, p. 17). In tempera on a densely woven, once-white silk satin, green leaves, blue, pink and orange flowers, thin branches and four different sorts of cockatoo are distributed in the spaces of an S-shaped brown thorny tendril. There is documentary evidence that the silks came from the Girard & Michelet and Isaac Bernhard factories, and were painted by the Isaac Joël and Sonnin & Bandow companies.

The Potsdam 'protected Jew' Isaac Joël manufactured wax-cloth wallpaper in Glienicke hunting lodge from 1758 onwards. On 18 February 1759, Friedrich Bogislaw von Tauentzien was ordered by Frederick II to issue an instruction to the General-direktorium in Berlin to draw up, without delay, a 'royal assurance' to the protected Jew and manufacturer Isaac Joël, in other words the deed of gift relating to the Glienicke hunting lodge. The lease of the former hunting lodge, together with its outbuildings, meadows and former pleasure garden, signed personally by the king, was however only drawn up five years later. It is dated Berlin, 6 September 1764, and attaches certain conditions

25a–b

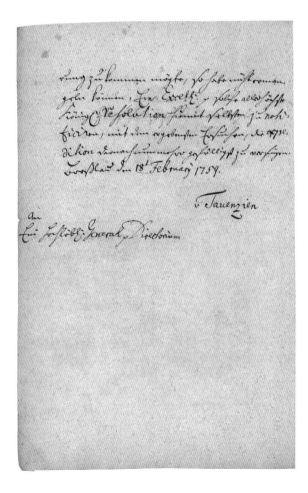

to the transfer. Thus Joël was to pay a yearly ground-rent of 12 talers to the Potsdam municipality, to maintain a plantation of 100 white mulberry trees, and above all, to keep the production of the wallpaper factory 'in a seemly condition'. IE/SK

26

Plan of Glienicke hunting lodge

Christian Ludwig Hildebrandt (Neumark c. 1720 – c. 1770 Graz) | Potsdam 1764 | Inscribed top right: 'Plan von dem ehemaligen Königl. Lustgarten und Zubehör in Glienicke ohnweit Potsdam' [plan of the former royal pleasure garden and appurtenances in Glienicke near Potsdam] | Ink on paper, colour wash, 36 x 44 cm | Potsdam, BLHA, Rep. 19 Steuerrat Potsdam, no. 3004 | Literature: Herzfeld 1993; exhib. cat. Königliche Visionen 2003

A truly princely factory location: the hunting lodge built by Philippe de Chièze in 1678 and altered by Charles Philippe

Dieussart in 1682. The three-storey main building offered plenty of space. The outbuildings and grounds facilitated a division of labour. Along with the location on the banks of the Havel and adjoining the road from Potsdam to Berlin, all this meant ideal conditions for the establishment of a waxcloth-wallpaper factory such as the protected Jew Isaac Levin Joël set up here in 1758. Shortly before, Frederick II had given him the property, which had suffered greatly through having been used as a military hospital for decades. When he accepted the gift of the hunting lodge, Joël also legally committed himself to plant and maintain a hundred mulberry trees. In the plan reproduced here, Hildebrandt has noted precisely what the king's gift to Joël actually included.

Frederick II was extraordinarily active in promoting the silk trade in Potsdam, and was at the same time one of the leading purchasers of silk products such as wall hangings, upholstery covers and curtains. In 1754 there were in Potsdam alone more than a hundred master craftsmen processing silk in some way, most of them being producers of velvet. Only they, and the silk-knitters, had organized themselves into a guild, while the silk-dyers and silk-embroiders remain unorganized. The list of silk textiles made in Potsdam ranged from upholstery covers, hair ribbons and stockings to wall hangings. The silk was of different sorts: velvet, plush, hatters' plush, satin, damask, gros de tour, as well a lightweight silk fabric, and in fibre blends. SK

27

Commode

Johann Friedrich Spindler (Bayreuth 1726–1799) and Heinrich Wilhelm Spindler (Bayreuth 1738–1788 Berlin) | Bayreuth c. 1760 | Pine, walnut, oak (body), walnut, maple, box and other woods (veneer and marquetry), bronze, iron, brass (fittings), 80 x 143 x 64.5 cm | Bayreuth, BSV, Neues Schloss, acquired with the support of the Ernst von Siemens Kunststiftung, BayNS.M0298, add. no.: BayNS.L-M0008 | Literature: Kreisel / Himmelheber 1983; Sangl 1991

This item of furniture documents the high standard of design, decor and workmanship achieved by the Spindlers at the court of Bayreuth. Their artistic and craft talents, enabling them to carry out large commissions in high quality, was doubtless the main reason for Frederick the Great to request them to collaborate in his building projects in Potsdam. The commode evinces the façade design typical of the Spindlers, namely the threefold structuring of the drawers: a larger, cambered central field is flanked by two cartouches. Unlike later commodes, the contours of the frames are extremely fine lines, and the central field contains not the then usual bouquet of flowers, but rather a figural, Arcadian composition, which skilfully exploits the natural structures of the wood used for the veneer. Its precise symbolism, like that on the pair of this commode in the Germanisches Nationalmuseum in Nuremberg, is still unexplained. JM

27

Wall mirror (Fig. 9, p. 23)

Johann August Nahl the Elder (Berlin 1710–1781 Kassel) | Berlin/Potsdam c. 1745 | Wood, carved, gilt frame, 125 x 70,0 cm | Eichenzell, HH, Schloss Fasanerie, inv. no. FAS M 3403 | Literature: Bleibaum 1933; Kreisel/Himmelheber 1983; exhib. cat. Hesse 2005

This mirror frame is a characteristic example of Nahl's art of unleashing a veritable pyrotechnic display of sculptural and ornamental movement in a very confined space. A symmetrical rectangular basic framework is here opened up in the corners by almost sketchy shell shapes which are connected to moulded bars. Above the top bar, decorated in the middle by an broad-petalled acanthus blossom, there are naturalistic flower-heads on the corner pieces, setting everything into wavelike motion. Like the crest of a wave, a large rocaille with wings towers up, and plays around a tendril of flowers.

The frame can be closely linked to Nahl's interior decoration in the Potsdam City Palace and in Sanssouci in c. 1745, so that we might reasonably date it to this period. It need not necessarily come from one of Frederick's palaces, however, but could have been made for one of Nahl's wealthy private clients.

The mirror once belonged to Ferdinand Robert-Tornow (1812–1875), who in the nineteenth century assembled one of the most important art collections in Berlin. He bequeathed the collection to the Crown Prince (later Kaiser Friedrich III) and his wife Victoria, the daughter of Queen Victoria. It comprised numerous antiques of regional provenance, collected as witnesses to Prussia's past. JM

29–32

Design for a long-case clock

Johann Michael Hoppenhaupt (Zittau 1709–1778/86 Merseburg) | Augsburg 1751/55 | Copper engraving, 31 x 17 cm | Potsdam, Potsdam Museum, inv. no. V81/587 K2

Armchair

Johann Christian Hoppenhaupt (Merseburg 1719–1778/86 Berlin | Potsdam 1755 | Limewood carved, gilded and painted, dark-blue wool velvet (early 20th c.), 120 x 86 x 73 cm | Potsdam, SPSG, inv. no. IV 354

Chair (Fig. 11, p. 25)

Johann Christian Hoppenhaupt | Potsdam 1755 | Limewood carved, gilded and painted, dark-blue wool velvet (early 20th c.), 116 x 65 x 73 cm | Potsdam, SPSG , inv. no. IV 356

Tabouret

Johann Christian Hoppenhaupt | Potsdam 1755 | Limewood carved, gilded and painted, dark-blue wool velvet (early 20th c.), 46 x 52 x 52 cm | Potsdam, SPSG, inv. no. IV 350

30

the typical furnishing style of the Potsdam court at this time, with its abundance of naturalistic elements. The items are in general more austere than Nahl's armchairs and chairs, which date from ten years earlier. They have little of the springy lightness and effervescence of the earlier pieces. The frames and outlines of the backs are quiet, and emphasized by coloured flowers in the middle; only in the legs, which converge towards the

32

Literature: Schreyer 1932; Kreisel/Himmelheber 1983

The brothers Johann Michael and Johann Christian Hoppenhaupt are among the most important and creative German craft sculptors of the Rococo. Their influence on Frederician furniture style can be seen above all in the king's commissions, carried out by their workshops, for room decorations and furnishings. Of particular importance, however, are a number of published design drawings by Johann Michael Hoppenhaupt, who had them engraved and printed, in a number of batches, by Johann Wilhelm Meil in Augsburg between 1751 and 1755. These numerous patterns, some of them executed for the New Palace ten years later, show, alongside wall patterns, also a number of console tables and various individual items of furniture, such as the long-case clock shown here. Individual elements of this design can be found in actually executed long-case clocks from the New Palace.

The armchair and tabouret belong to a suite of furniture from Frederick the Great's study in the Potsdam City Palace. That they were made in Johann Christian Hoppenhaupt's workshop is documented by Manger, who attributed all of the decorative carving in the room (furnished in 1755) to him. Both the decoration of the study and its carved furniture bear witness to

floor in a manner reminiscent of a dancer, does Hoppenhaupt allow himself an almost abruptly vehement accentuation in the form of bulging, armour-like ornamentation. JM

33

Lidded vase, lid missing

Constantin Philipp Georg Sartori factory (Charlottenburg 1747–1812 Charlottenburg), sign. 'P' | Potsdam c. 1780/90 | Faience, high-fired polychrome painting on white ground, 36.5 cm (height), 16 cm (diameter of foot), 10 cm (diameter of neck) | Potsdam, Potsdam Museum, inv. no. V 78/19 Fa | Literature: Mauter/Peibst 1993; exhib. cat. Königliche Visionen 2003; Mauter 2008

On the death of the founder of the factory, Christian Friedrich Rewendt, in 1768, the business was bequeathed to his sons Friedrich Wilhelm and Johann Christian Rewendt. The latter took over the sole running of the business in 1770, but proved to be incapable, from the point of view both of character and competence, of putting it on its feet; sales were simply inadequate. Debts mounted up, the city council executed distraints, and finally in 1775 the creditors drove the firm into bankruptcy. On 8 April of the same year, the sculptor and stucco plasterer

Constantin Philipp Georg Sartori acquired the factory, and with true business acumen led the company to renewed prosperity.

In September 1775 Sartori's foreman Johann Gottfried Reinicke, who had previously worked in the meanwhile insolvent Lüdicke factory in Berlin, began to write his 'Potsdamer Glasur- und Farbenbuch' ('Potsdam Book of Glazes and Paints'), which is still highly thought of in specialist circles. A second part followed from 1785. Completed in 1795, the work, now kept in the Märkisches Museum in Berlin, ultimately included recipes for 56 glazes and 86 paints. It also contains references to numerous experiments with new ceramic materials, for example stoneware, as well as glazed and unglazed surfaces. In this way Sartori sought to broaden the company's product range in order to maintain the factory's competitiveness. It is also in this context, though, that the introduction of new shapes and painted decorations must be seen. The lidded vase shows that around 1780, alongside the still-popular Rococo motifs, Neo-classical elements were coming to the fore; their models were mostly to be found in contemporary porcelain wares. TS

34

Two lacquered vases with lids

Probably from the Constantin Philipp Georg Sartori factory (Charlottenburg 1747–1812 Charlottenburg) | Probably Potsdam, late 18th c. | Papier-mâché (body and lid), wood (handle and base), black-and-gold chinoiserie lacquering | Vase 1: 35.3 cm (height), 1.5 x 12.9 x 13 cm (base); vase 2: 36.6 cm (height), 1.6 x 13.2 x 12.9 cm (base) | Private collection, Berlin | Literature: Nicolai repr. 1993; Thieme-Becker 1907ff., vol. 18, p. 477; cat. no. 220–222, p. 174f.; Stengel 1958; Mauter 1996; Richter 2005, p. 136f., ill. 115; Stobwasser

We know from Friedrich Nicolai and his Beschreibung der königlichen Residenzstadt Potsdam [Description of the Royal Residence City of Potsdam] that in the Rewendt faience factory which he took over in 1775, Konstantin Georg Philipp Sartori also made 'vases in all sorts of shapes and sizes, gilded and lacquered in the latest taste'. In addition to papier-mâché, the material used may also have been a plaster-of-Paris mixture.

The cylindrical bodies and the lids of the two black-lacquered lidded vases painted in the Chinese style are each made of a lightweight grey papier-mâché mass. The angular handles and flat square bases, typical of the period around 1800, are of wood. The reddish-gold lacquer painting shows, on the larger of the two vases, a heron with dragonflies, and on the rear and the lid, Asiatic houses on stilts on a lake. Delicate swags frame the body of the vase and the round foot. The handles, the sides of the base, the pommel of the lid, and various bulges are painted gold. The second vase, additionally, shows a Chinese man with an exotic bird on a tether. Following the great economic success of lacquerware made by the firm of Stobwasser based in Berlin and Braunschweig, numerous copycat products found their way on to the market. Alongside boxes, cases, vessels, vases and small furniture items made of papier-mâché, pewter vessels were also lacquered and elaborately painted. IE

35

Lidded tureen

Christian Friedrich Rewendt factory (1704–1768 Potsdam), signed 'P/R' | Potsdam 1754–1775 | Faience, high-fired manganese purple painting on white ground with whitish-grey glaze, 34 x 34.5 x 24 cm | Potsdam, Kunsthandlung Seidel & Sohn | Literature: Fuchs/Heiland 1925; Mauter/Peibst 1993, p. 215

The very special form of this tureen, which rests on four 'paws', and whose high lid in the form of an upturned sea-shell ends in a long-drawn-out and turned-in handle, was, according to Paul Heiland, probably based on a model produced by the famous Strasbourg faience factory operated by Paul Hannong, where it was listed under shape number 429. As the Strasbourg factory also employed artists and technicians from the porcelain factories in Meissen and Hoechst, it cannot be ruled out that this shape came originally from there. In particular, Count Brühl's swan service, made in Meissen between 1737 and 1742, included a number of display tureens in the form of shells resting on four paw-shaped feet, and these may have served as models. With certain modifications, the tureen shape created in Strasbourg gradually spread via the faience factories in Höchst, Crailsheim, Nuremberg and Münden all the way to Berlin, and from there probably made its way to Rheinsberg and Potsdam too. Heiland already pointed out that in the course of this dissemination process, the original appearance of the basic form, decorated with rocaille shape and with ornamen-

tation under the edge of the lid, was largely lost. What he meant by this can also be seen in this tureen, namely that the painting, with scattered manganese-purple flowers, 'takes no account of the (once doubtless maritime) form and totally misunderstands the purpose of the moulded decorations'. A similar piece, probably from the Lüdicke factory, is described by Mauter and Peibst. TS

Potsdam after and in Remembrance of Frederick

Even in Frederick's lifetime, Potsdam was a magnet for tourists. Petitioners, admirers, and the simply curious came from all over Europe. The king's death did not put an end to this flow of visitors. On the contrary, authentic sites such as his summer palace, Sanssouci, or his tomb in the Garrison Church became places of pilgrimage. Thus the king put his stamp on the city not just as someone who commissioned new buildings; he became for Potsdam, his residence and garrison city, its figure of destiny.

In the nineteenth century his successors on the Prussian throne continued the composition of the cityscape, with its palaces and gardens. Frederick William IV in particular sought through his 'Triumphal Road' project to commemorate his illustrious predecessor by carrying on Frederick the Great's work. At the same time, the Hohenzollerns commissioned Frederick the Great memorials.

Prussian military tradition and the cult of Frederick also proved fateful for Potsdam though. Thus in 1933, having just come to power, the Nazis exploited the city and the Garrison Church as a backdrop for their 'Potsdam Day'. After the war, this 'spirit of Potsdam' became the chief excuse for the demolition of Frederician heritage objects. Today, Frederick is once again an important ambassador for the Potsdam brand. IE

Frederick II's Death

Bernhard Rode (Berlin 1725–1797 Berlin), completed by Eberhard Henne (Gunsleben 1759–1828) | Berlin 1792 | Etching, 42.5 x 62 cm (panel), 40 x 60.5 cm (image) | Inscribed, bottom left: gemahlt und geätzt von B. Rode/zu finden bey E. Henne und bey Heinr. Aug. Henne in Berlin [painted and etched by B. Rode/can be found at E. Henne and Heinr. Aug. Henne in Berlin]; bottom right: vollendet von E. Henne [completed by E. Henne]; bottom centre: Friedrichs II. Tod [Frederick II's Death] | Potsdam, Potsdam Museum, inv. no. 86/1668 K2

Frederick the Second's Arrival in Elysium

G. W. Hoffmann (18th c.), Christian von Mechel (1737–1817) and Bartholomäus Hübner (1727–after 1795) | Basel 1788 | Inscribed: Friedrich des Zweiten Ankunft im Elisium/Allen wahren Verehrern dieses großen Monarchen gewidmet/von Johann Andreas Kunze [Frederick II's Arrival in Elysium/Dedicated to all true devotees of this great monarch/by Johann Andreas Kunze], bottom left: G: W: Hoffmann delineavit Be-

rolini; bottom centre: Chr: a Mechel Sculptur: direxit; bottom right: B: Hübner sculpsit Basileae 1788 | Copper engraving: 38 x 51.2 cm (image), 46.5 x 54.5 cm (sheet) | Potsdam, Potsdam Museum, inv. no. 82/1662 K2

Literature: Thieme-Becker 1907ff., vol. 17, p. 255 (Hoffmann), Thieme-Becker 1907ff., vol. 18, p. 44 (Hübner); Seidel 1910; Jacobs 1990, p. 309, no. 149; exhib. cat. Friedrich der Große 2012, cat. no. 2.15, p. 45

The death of Frederick II created a broad echo in Prussia and the whole of Europe. Bernhard Rode presented his version of Frederick the Great's death scene at the Berlin Academy exhibition in 1787. In 1792 Eberhard Henne produced a print of the painting. The image reveals that Rode knew the circumstances of Frederick II's death, but was not familiar with the room in which he died and which had been altered in the year of his death. Frederick the Great had died in an armchair in his bedroom in Sanssouci at 2.20 a.m. on 17 August 1787 in the

FRIEDRICH DES ZWEITEN ANKUNFT IM ELISIUM

presence of his physician Christian Gottlieb Selle, the two adjutants Neumann and Schöning, as well as a few lackeys. Minister von Hertzberg and lieutenant general Count von Görz, as well as the king's nephew and successor, Frederick William II, arrived in the palace shortly afterwards, or at around 3 a.m. In an idealized Neo-classical room with the fire going, the doctor feels the pulse of the king who has just peacefully passed away. The clock behind him reads 3 a.m. To the right, by a table overloaded with books and plans, four surprised gentlemen become witnesses to the scene. Rode was presumably depicting the adjutants, minister Hertzberg and Count von Görz here.

The work *Frederick the Second's Arrival in Elysium*, published in Basel in 1788, shows the king being taken across the river Styx to the mythical Greek island of heroes and sons of gods by Charon the ferryman. He is greeted by heroes of the Antiquity as well as by his father Frederick William I and his great-great-grandfather the Great Elector. On the left-hand side of the picture, generals Zieten, Seydlitz and Schwerin are hurrying over. IE

38

Statuette of Frederick II with two Italian greyhounds

Johann Gottfried Schadow (Berlin 1764 – 1850 Berlin) | Berlin c. 1822 | Bronze, 90.5 cm (height), 32 cm (depth), 39 cm (width of the plinth) | Potsdam, SPSG, Skulpturensammlung, inv. no. 1375 (GK III 3938) | Literature: Bloch / Grzimek 1994; Maaz 1994, cat. no. 38, p. 215f.; Hüneke 1997/98

As a Berlin sculptor at the end of the Rococo and start of the Neo-classical period, Johann Gottfried Schadow shaped like no one else the image of Frederick the Great in sculpture. He actively participated in the discussions and suggestions about a monument for the Prussian king after the latter's death. Commissioned by minister Hertzberg, Schadow also produced the earliest public memorial to Frederick. It was erected in Stettin [now Sczcecin] in 1793. The statuette of Frederick II with two greyhounds is remarkable in several respects. It was not a commissioned work. It was sculpted by Schadow in 1821/22 as a mere 'pastime', to see 'what kind of an impact such a figure would have', Schadow wrote to his son Ridolfo on 1 September 1821. He himself called it 'prosaic'. Frederick is depicted between his two Italian greyhounds Alkmene and Hasenfuss, wearing a tricorne and holding a cane, capturing him in a private moment, as it were. The anecdotal 'human' image of the king became very widespread from 1840 onward as a result of the depictions by Adolph Menzel. Maybe that explains why the statuette, which had not initially been very successful, also became very popular from 1840 onwards, the centenary of Frederick the Great's accession to the throne, whereupon it was reproduced many times. Frederick William IV also liked the piece and acquired it in 1841 for the study-bedroom of Frederick the Great in Sanssouci, a room whose reconstruction he had commissioned. IE

39

Music stand belonging to the Empress Frederick (Princess Victoria)

Franz Borchmann and Carl Heinrich Preetz, after Melchior Kambly, 1767 | Berlin/Potsdam c. 1890 | Oak (?), mother-of-pearl, tortoiseshell, bronze, 176 x 45 cm (stand), 34 x 53.1 x 47.5 cm (rest for the music) | Fulda, HH, Schloss Fasanerie Eichenzell, inv. no. FAS M 1954 | Literature: Seidel 1901; Nicht 1973, cat. no. 7, p. 9; Kreisel/Himmelheber 1983, cat. no. 809, p. 416, fig. 809

This replica of a Frederician music stand from the workshop of Johann Melchior Kambly was commissioned by the Empress Frederick in 1890, probably for the Friedrichshof in Kronberg in the Taunus, which was built as her widowhood residence. The copy was made by the court furniture maker and supplier Franz Borchmann, who worked at Am Kanal 23 in Potsdam between 1884 and 1922, and his colleague, Carl Heinrich Preetz, the court metalworker, who worked in Berlin at Friedrichstrasse 63 between 1888 and 1906. Both made pieces in 1888 for Kaiser Frederick (Friedrich III) during his brief reign, and later for Kaiser Wilhelm II. In a letter dated 18 January 1889, Borchmann asks 'to be considered favourably when commissions for the furniture at Friedrichskron (hof)' were given. At the Paris World Exposition of 1900, the two court purveyors exhibited a number of replicas of Baroque furniture which had been commissioned by Wilhelm II. The Kambly music stand, of which two originals from the Music Rooms in the Potsdam City Palace and in Sanssouci survive to this day in the collection of the Stiftung Preussische Schösser und Gärten, bears witness to the great value attached in the late nineteenth century to objects associated with Frederick II. IE

39

40–42

Cover of the magazine *Die Woche*
Der Tag von Potsdam ('Potsdam Day')

Vol. 35, special issue on 21 March 1933 | Printed on paper, 32.2 x 24.7 cm | Potsdam, Potsdam Museum, inv. no. B-2012-328

Cover of the magazine *Die Woche*
Der Geist von Potsdam ('The Spirit of Potsdam')

Issue 15, 15 April 1933 | Printed on paper, 32.2 x 23.5 cm | Potsdam, Potsdam Museum, inv. no. B-2012-449

Poem *Potsdam I*

Heinrich Anacker (Buchs, Kanton Aargau 1901–1971 Wasserburg am Bodensee) | From: *Die Fanfare. Gedichte der Deutschen Erhebung*, München 1933, pp. 92 f. | Letterpress, bound, 18.5 x 13.3 cm | Berlin, SBB PK, inv. no. Yo 39900

The ceremonial activities in Potsdam on 21 March 1933 to mark the opening of the German Reichstag were reported in detail on the radio, in the daily newspapers and in magazines. The old Prussian military and garrison city had only been selected as a venue for the events because of the Reichstag fire in Berlin. But this makeshift solution quickly turned out to be a propagandist stroke of fortune.

The Prussian spirit and military tradition were evoked in the locations associated with Frederick the Great, his summer residence Sanssouci and his tomb in the Garrison Church. The cover of the magazine *Die Woche* on Potsdam Day (cat. 40) also features a typical image of 'Old Fritz' in old age against the silhouette of the Garrison Church. This cover was designed by Klaus Richer for the Scherl Verlag. This a publishing house, founded in Halle in 1900, had changed hands in 1916, the new owner being the right-wing media mogul Alfred Hugenberg, who, since the 1920s, had been one of the most important supporters of the Nazis and helped them achieve popularity. One month later, in issue 15, published on 15 April 1933, 'The Spirit of Potsdam' appeared on the cover: a watercolour spring picture of Sanssouci during the magnolia blossom (cat. 41). Dr Alfred Hugenberg, whom Hitler had included in his cabinet as the minister for economic affairs, agriculture and food, started his editorial with the sentence: 'The German nation has found its way to Potsdam.' The atmosphere of change celebrated here, which was in the spirit of the supposed continuation of the Frederician authoritarian, military state tradition, corresponded to the flowering magnolia tree against the backdrop of Sanssouci.

In the same spirit, the chief Nazi poet Heinrich Anacker from southern Germany also wrote three poems about Potsdam Day (cat. 42). They were published in 1933 in the anthology *Die Fanfare. Gedichte der Deutschen Erhebung* ('The Fan-

40

The people of Potsdam did not ask whether friends and colleagues had been to see the play, but how many times. The venue had room for 600 spectators and was always sold out. The comedy, which was first performed at the Volkstheater Rostock in 1981, was a humorous and critical commentary on the newly erupted 'heritage debate' in East Germany. Martin Luther and Frederick the Great were critically interviewed by the 'examination institute for the reintegration of historical figures'. The racy production, loaded with provocative quips about everyday life in East Germany, addressed many a grievance of 'real existing socialism'. Incredibly bold punch lines, such as 'If you don't obey, you'll be sent to Hegel Avenue', which were immediately associated with the Potsdam headquarters of the Stasi, the Ministry for State Security, contributed to the production's legendary reputation.

The theatre staff working with Eckhard Becker and the dramaturge Michael Philipps chose the beer bottle label of the 'Rex Pils' Spezial by the VEB Brauerei Potsdam (the publicly owned brewery) for the title motif for the programme and the poster. Since around 1981 it had featured a grenadier from the Frederician Grenadier Guard 6th Battalion. This fitted the play's contents and the new ease with which the people of Potsdam could face Frederick the Great once again. The programme's photographs were also remarkable. They showed the actor playing Frederick, Klaus Schöneberg, in costume, standing outside the Museum für Deutsche Geschichte (Museum of German History), in front of the memorial to Frederick on Unter den Linden, at the tomb in Sanssouci, which was still empty, but also (and particularly provocatively) on the site of the demolished Potsdam City Palace and at the inner-German border by the Brandenburg Gate in Berlin. IE

fare. Poems of Germany's Exaltation'), published by Franz Eber Nachfolger in Munich. This volume, which contained 92 poems subdivided into categories such as 'persecuted and forbidden', 'the soldier sings' and 'persevere, ready for the final battle!', was dedicated to Adolf Hitler and is a poetic compendium of Nazi history and ideology. IE

43–44

Theatre poster *Die Preussen kommen* ('The Prussians are Coming') for the production in the Hans-Otto-Theater
Potsdam 1983 | 40 x 57 cm | Potsdam, Potsdam Museum, inv. no. 2009 P 5314

Programme *Die Preussen kommen* ('The Prussians are Coming') for the production in the Hans-Otto-Theater
Potsdam 1983 | 18.6 x 20.6 cm | Potsdam, Potsdam Museum, inv. no. V 2603/10 S

The play Die Preussen kommen, written by Claus Hamme and staged in 1983 by Eckhard Becker, is still one of the greatest successes of the Hans-Otto-Theater. After the première on 20 February 1983 in the old venue in Zimmerstrasse (the former community centre 'Zum Alten Fritz'), the play had a run of 205 performances, a figure that remains unsurpassed to this day.

44

Frederick and Potsdam in Modern Art

The conceptual triangle Frederick – Potsdam – Modernism seems at first sight not to join up. While the king had a definitive role in shaping 'his' city, the effects on modern art are anything but self-evident.

And yet there are numerous links with and references to Frederick and Frederician Potsdam in the art of the twentieth and twenty-first centuries. The artistic reception of Frederick II, which was largely formed by Adolph Menzel in the nineteenth century, underwent a translation into the formal language of Modernism with Lovis Corinth, a member of the Berlin Secession. His 1921/22 portfolio *Fridericus Rex* forms the opener for a cabinet of graphic art that leads via the Leipzig artist Bernhard Heisig all the way to Claudia Berg. At the focus is the endeavour to capture the complex personality of the king, which oscillates between the opposing poles of warmonger on the one hand and Enlightenment philosopher on the other.

The art of the present day focuses on Frederician Potsdam, for example when Frederick's lying in state in Sanssouci or the millennium celebration are put into pictures. In addition, downtown Potsdam, where to this day Frederick the Great's architecture survives, or else, as in the Alter Markt, is being re-created through reconstruction, serves as a source of artistic inspiration. JG

45 a–c

Three sheets from the 47-part cycle *Fridericus Rex*: title sheet, *Portrait of Voltaire* and *The Dying Frederick* from the portfolio *From the Life of Frederick the Great*

Lovis Corinth (Tapiau [now Gvardeysk] 1858–1925 Zandvoort) | 1921/22 | Colour lithographs, each 32 x 26 cm, Verlag Fritz Gurlitt | Inscribed: Fridericus Rex (1, bottom centre); Voltaire (2, bottom centre); La montagne est passée, 17 August 1786 (3, top right) | Berlin, SMB PK, Kupferstichkabinett, inv. no. 74-1985, 74-1985/11 and 74-1985/26 | Literature: exhib. cat. Lovis Corinths Fridericus Rex 1986; exhib. cat. Friedrich der Große 1986b; Kohle 2001

The cycle *Fridericus Rex* was initiated by a meeting between Lovis Corinth and Paul Eipper, the head of production and chief editor of the art publisher Fritz Gurlitt, on 19 November 1920. The commission for a graphics portfolio was connected with a visit by Corinth to the Zeughaus in Berlin, which became, for him, an artistic inspiration: 'Imagine, I enter a room, and there stands a blue uniform, a tricorne, a cane, I see this from some way off, not very clearly, and immediately think, that must be Frederick the Great, truly, and as I got nearer, there it was: his clothes. […] Just as well the museum had not had any wax heads made. Like this it looked so much more real!'

Unlike Adolf Menzel, Lovis Corinth, an artist of the Berlin Secession, was less interested in Frederick II as an historical personage, and thus not in a juxtaposition of allegedly historical scenes either. His cycle arose as an expression of personal feeling; scenes and individual depictions were reduced to their essentials and sketched directly in rapid strokes, and thus translated into a modern formal canon.

The French philosopher Voltaire is one of the few people in the royal circle to have been honoured with a portrait in Corinth's cycle. The artist translated his intellectual potency into rapid, impulsive strokes that depict Voltaire twice, as 'a picture within a picture'.

Lovis Corinth, who studied Frederick II's death-mask intensively, used it in two ways in the cycle. In the penultimate picture it served him as the model for his depiction of the king on his death-bed, while at the end of the sequence, in King Frederick and his Circle, it was included as a profile view, entitled 'Death Mask'. JG

46–47

Frederick the Great (Frontispiece)

Bernhard Heisig (Breslau [now Wrocław] 1925–2011 Strohdehne an der Havel) | In: Sechs Weggefährten, [Six Comrades in Arms], luxury edition of the catalogue with two lithographs (Frederick the Great), Brusberg Kabinettdruck 9, Berlin 1997 | Lithograph, 23 x 15 cm | Potsdam, Potsdam Museum, inv. no.. Bk-2012-5

Frederick

Bernhard Heisig | 2009 | Oil on canvas, 50 x 60 cm | Brusberg private collection

Literature: exhib. cat. Heisig 2003; exhib. cat. Heisig 2005; Heisig 2005; Beaucamp 2010; Sperling 2010

Bernhard Heisig was the 'greatest moralist in contemporary art', or so he was called by Eduard Beaucamp in the catalogue published to mark the artist's 85th birthday in 2010. No other painter so comprehensively confronted German history, guilt, aberration and human ensnarement. His themes range from the Prussian danse macabre, across the Bismarck era and the madness of the Second World War, right up to the present day.

In his late work, Heisig approaches the ambivalent personality of Frederick II in a positively depth-psychological manner, inspecting the contradictory stages in the life of the Prussian king. The very different depictions of the king reflect the painter's changing view of Frederick II's personal destiny in the context of German history; sometimes the features of the king come across in the manner of a Corinth, striking, brooding, and challenging; sometimes, especially in Heisig's last oils, they remain an indefinable, fragmentary approach that arrestingly reflects not only the inner conflicts of the monarch, but also the misuse of the mythologized personality to the point of unrecognizability. The half-length portrait dating from 2009 indicates the identity of the king only through the blue dress uniform of the 1st Battalion of Guards, the tricorne, and the orange sash of the Order of the Eagle.

Heisig seems less interested in the king's outward appearance than in his emotional state and the contradictory nature of his actions. In addition to the oil paintings, from the 1990s he also created numerous lithographs portraying Frederick II. Conspicuous in every case is his orientation to the aging king, with striking, haggard features, sometimes bare-headed, leaning on his stick, without any hint of royal dignity. Like Lovis Corinth, Heisig too succeeds in his confrontation with the king's hardening physiognomy, in which the future death mask seems to be shining through even during his lifetime. The 1997 lithograph seems to have been used once again by Heisig for the 2001–2003 oil study *The Great King*. JG

48

Frederick of Prussia

Claudia Berg (b. Halle an der Saale, 1976) | Halle 2012 | Original artist's book with five hand-printed drypoint etchings on rag paper, four pages of text with title and colophon | 35 x 27 cm (sheet); Kleist: 11.9 x 7.8 cm (plate); Lessing: 12 x 9.6 cm (plate); Friedrich II.: 12 x 9.8 cm (plate); Voltaire: 12.1 x 9.7 cm (plate); Kant: 11.9 x 9.6 cm (plate) | Potsdam, Potsdam Museum, inv. no. BK-2012-3 | Literature: Müller 1977; Berg 2005

hard-won liberation of philosophy. A central passage in Müller's play opens the text on the series of portraits: 'If intellectuals push into the centre of things, they lose the power to make changes. They must remain on the fringe, work on the fringe. From the centre, it is impossible to achieve anything. It's government officials who belong in the centre.' The following texts are devoted to the selected intellectual circle, and supplement the view of the portraits.

That of Frederick II is based on the well-known 1781 portrait by Anton Graff, which shows him with a powdered wig and simple uniform jacket as well as the 'military insignia' of the Order of the Black Eagle. In Claudia Berg's etching, Frederick has been deliberately shown laterally reversed, the profile is more pointed, the expression has been made more cynical, in keeping with the accompanying text, which draws a psychological picture of the king. Each portrait is the result of an intensive confrontation on the artist's part with the 'sitter', his appearance, personality and influence being given attention in equal measure. Her great sensitivity of approach led her to revise each copperplate a number of times. JG

49

Sanssouci – Sanssouci

Matthias Koeppel (b. Hamburg 1937) | Berlin 1993 | Oil on canvas, 200 x 300 cm | Private collection | Literature: Christoffel 1997, pp. 35–37

48

The artist Claudia Berg has produced, specially for this exhibition, an original artist's book with five drypoint etchings and selected texts. Inspired by conversations with her former mentor Helmut Brade, who was responsible for the graphic design for the production of Heiner Müller's play *Leben Gundlings, Friedrich von Preussen, Lessings Schlaf Traum Schrei* at the Berliner Ensemble, Claudia Berg confronted Frederick II's relationship with the intellectual elite of his country. As is well known, the francophile king was in contact with the philosopher and Enlightenment figure Voltaire, but he was ill-informed about important German-speaking figures in literature and philosophy, as is demonstrated by his 1780 treatise *De la littérature allemande* (1780).

With her five portrait etchings, Claudia Berg developed an artistic concept for the intellectual history of the late eighteenth century that has never been attempted in this form: she extends the historic circle centring on Frederick and Voltaire by including Immanuel Kant, Gotthold Ephraim Lessing and Heinrich von Kleist. The fact that Kleist was born too late ever to have met Frederick in person is of no great import for this series: what links the writer to the king is his involuntary conscription into the Prussian military in Potsdam, and the

Matthias Koeppel, who founded the 'School of New Magnificence' in 1973 along with Johannes Grützke, Manfred Bluth and Karlheinz Ziegler, is one of the most important Realist artists of today. Furthermore, he is a pictorial chronicler of German history. Koeppel chose two significant events in Potsdam as his subjects in the early 1990s. His paintings were created as a snapshot of Frederick the Great's lying-in-state in Sanssouci on 17 August 1991, and on the occasion of the Potsdam millennial celebrations in 1993.

The large panel painting made for the city's historic anniversary was created at the suggestion of the then chief executive of the city, Helmut Przybilski. As a motif for the millennial celebrations, Matthias Koeppel chose the Sanssouci world heritage site, and placed Frederick the Great and his court on the left of the diptych, with representatives of national, regional and local politics on the right.

Two realities are thus contrasted on two panels; namely the time of Frederick the Great and the present as-was in 1993. They are joined through the shared evening sky over Sanssouci. On the left Frederick is depicted in civilian clothing, wearing the badge of the Order of the Black Eagle, hat in hand: a depiction alluding to a late portrait of the king by Johann Heinrich Christoph Francke. Surrounding him are the Count of

Schwerin, court composer Carl Heinrich Graun, and Voltaire. On the right, we see a figure viewed from behind, provocatively sporting a Mohican hair style. On this figure are focused the eyes of President Richard von Weizsäcker, Chancellor Helmut Kohl and Mayor Horst Gramlich. He could not have expressed the omnipresence of Frederick's legacy in Potsdam any more concisely. JG

50

Potsdam Spins

Anna Werkmeister (b. Dingelstädt, Eichsfeld/Thüringen 1949) | Potsdam 2012 | Video installation with portrait bust of Frederick the Great | 3 monitors, video sequences of 1:30 min | Private collection, SPSG | Literature: exhib. cat. Turning Points 2004

With her video installation *Potsdam Spins*, Anna Werkmeister brings together past and present on imagined equal terms. The relationships between state and individual, status and tolerance in society are also central themes in this confrontation. A bust of Frederick the Great, based to Johannes Eckstein's portrait of the ruler, itself based on the death-mask, illustrates the view of the Prussian king by an unknown twen-

tieth-century artist. The statuesque sternness of his life-size image is contrasted with individual body movements, which develop their dynamics with recurring motions. In contrast to the traditional bust, the spins do not focus on facial features, but capture rhythm, posture, repetition, duration and change of individual momentum as rhythmic structures, which appear to approach each other but then disappear inexorably from the field of view of the viewer. With *Potsdam Spins* and the selection of the protagonists displayed therein, Anna Werkmeister points to art and culture not least as an all-embracing interface between Frederick's Potsdam and the modern city. After all, it is individual citizens, especially those from the city's cultural institutions, who render outstanding services to its historic heritage – and at the same time retain their focus on current developments. BM

51

Frederick between Chance and Necessity

Rainer Gottemeier (b. Potsdam 1949) | Potsdam 2012 | 28 alu-dibond neon cases with 158 letters, two neo silhouettes of Frederick II, 15.2 x 0.3 m | Potsdam, Potsdam Museum | Literature: Gottemeier 2007; Gottemeier 2010

Potsdam-based light-artist Rainer Gottemeier developed an artistic design for the façade of the new museum building for the tercentenary of the birth of Frederick the Great, and thus created the only external exhibit of the exhibition.

Rainer Gottemeier studied the texts of Frederick the Great intensely before choosing a quote rich in associations for the light exhibit with which he confronts the public. *Between Chance and Necessity* is its title, which refers to Frederick the Great as captain of his ship of state. In full the quotation is as follows: 'The authoritative law of necessity forced me to leave much to chance, to behave like a pilot who has put himself at the mercy of the wind rather than follow the instructions of his compass.'

The quotation receives its physical frame of reference in the attic zone of the museum in the City Hall opposite the City Palace, built under Frederick the Great by Christian Ludwig Hillebrandt and Jan Bouman between 1753 and 1755. By way of this quote Frederick symbolically appears in the urban setting of the Alter Markt, which, following his alterations to the residence in 1744, he gradually turned into a place reminiscent of an Italian piazza; in so doing he communicates his actions to passers-by, the citizens of Potsdam, and visitors from around the world.

The quote is determined by two important terms in cultural history: 'chance' and 'necessity'. On the one hand they stand for freedom and risk, on the other for determination and security. Frederick operates between these two poles, and solicits trust. According to his statement, he will bring about strategically clever actions even in complex situations. The immediate reference to the allegories of virtue of the attic storey by Gottlieb Heymüller, amongst them vigilance, steadfastness and fairness, endow the quote with conviction. JG

Appendix

Bibliography

EXHIBITION CATALOGUES

Exhib. cat.Friederisiko 2012
Friederisiko. Friedrich der Große, SPSG
(eds.), 2 vols., Munich 2012 (Catalogue
of the exhibition in the Neues Palais, Potsdam, 28 April – 28 October 2012)

Exhib. cat. Friedrich der Große 1986a
Friedrich der Große, Friedrich Benning-
hoven, Helmut Börsch-Supan and Iselin
Gundermann (eds.), Berlin 1986 (Catalogue of the exhibition of the GStA PK to
mark the 200th anniversary of the death
of King Friedrich II of Prussia)

Exhib. cat. Friedrich der Große 1986b
Friedrich der Große. Sein Bild im Wandel
der Zeiten, Wolfgang J. Kaiser (ed.), Frankfurt am Main 1986 (Catalogue of the
exhibition in the Historisches Museum
Frankfurt am Main, 12 November 1986 –
15 February 1987)

Exhib. cat. Friedrich der Große 2012
Friedrich der Große – verehrt, verklärt, ver-
dammt, Deutsches Historisches Museum
(ed.), Stuttgart 2012 (Catalogue of the
exhibition in the DHM, 21 March – 26 August 2012)

**Exhib. cat. Friedrich II. und
die Kunst 1986**
Friedrich II. und die Kunst, Generaldirektion
der Staatlichen Schlösser und Gärten Potsdam-Sanssouci (eds.), compiled by Hans-
Joachim Giersberg, Potsdam 1986 (Catalogue of the exhibition in the Neues Palais,
Potsdam, 19 July – 12 October 1986)

Exhib. cat. Heisig 2003
Brusberg, Dieter: Bernhard Heisig "Gestern
und in unserer Zeit", Berlin 2003 (Catalogue of the exhibition in the Galerie Brusberg Berlin, 6 September – 15 November
2003)

Exhib. cat. Heisig 2005
Bernhard Heisig. Wut der Bilder, Eckhart
Gillen (ed.), Cologne 2005 (Catalogue of
the exhibition in the Museum der Bildenden Künste Leipzig, 20 March – 29 May
2005, in K20 Kunstsammlung Nordrhein-
Westfalen, Düsseldorf, 11 June – 29 September 2005 and in the Nationalgalerie,
SMB, 22 October 2005 – 30 January 2006)

Exhib. cat. Hesse 2005
Hesse, a Princely German Collection, Pene-
lope Hunter-Stiebel (ed.), Oregon 2005
(Catalogue of the exhibition in the Portland
Art Museum, 29 October 2005 – 19 March
2006)

Exhib. cat. Ideal City 2007
Ideal City – Invisible Cities, Sabrina van der
Ley and Markus Richter (eds.), Frankfurt am
Main 2006 (Catalogue of the exhibition in
Zamość, 18 June – 22 August 2006 and in
Potsdam, 9 September – 29 October 2006)

Exhib. cat. Knobelsdorff 1999
Zum Maler und zum großen Architekten
geboren. Georg Wenzeslaus von Knobels-
dorff 1699–1753, Tilo Eggeling and Ute-
G. Weickardt (eds.), Berlin/Potsdam 1999
(Catalogue of the exhibition in the Weißer
Saal of Schloss Charlottenburg, Berlin,
18 February – 25 April 1999)

Exhib. cat. Königliche Visionen 2003
Königliche Visionen. Potsdam eine Stadt in
der Mitte Europas, Potsdam Museum (ed.),
Potsdam 2003 (Catalogue of the exhibition
in the Kutschstall am Neuen Markt, 30 August 2003 – 28 March 2004)

**Exhib. cat. Lovis Corinths Fridericus Rex
1986**
Lovis Corinths Fridericus Rex. Der Preußen-
könig in Mythos und Geschichte, Hans
Gerhard Hanessen (ed.), Berlin 1986
(Catalogue of the exhibition in the Kupfer-

stichkabinett Berlin SMB PK, 27 February –
20 April 1986, in the Wissenschaftszent-
rum Bonn-Bad Godesberg, 7 May – 15 June
1986 and in Schloß Cappenberg, 2 July –
24 August 1986)

Exhib. cat. Nordskulptur:licht 2007
Nordskulptur:licht, Verein zur Förderung
der Kunst in Neumünster e. V. (ed.), Neumünster 2007 (Catalogue of the exhibition
in Neumünster, Sager Viertel and public
space, 2 – 18 November 2007)

Exhib. cat. Paradies des Rokoko 1998
Galli Bibiena und der Museumshof der
Wilhelmine von Bayreuth, Peter O. Krück-
mann (ed.), vol. 2, Munich/New York 1998
(Catalogue of the exhibition of the BSV,
21 April – 27 September 1998)

Exhib. cat. La Roma di Piranesi 2006
La Roma di Piranesi. La città del Settecento
nelle Grandi Vedute, Mario Bevilaqua and
Mario Gori Sassoli (eds.), Rome 2006 (Catalogue of the exhibition in the Museo del Corso,
14 November 2006 – 25 February 2007)

Exhib. cat. Sammeln 2009
Privates und öffentliches Sammeln in Potsdam. 100 Jahre "Kunst ohne König", Potsdam Museum and Potsdamer Kunstverein
e. V. (ed.), Berlin 2009 (Catalogue of the
exhibition in HBPG 15 May - 2 August 2009)

Exhib. cat. Textile Kostbarkeiten 1993
Textile Kostbarkeiten – in Sanssouci be-
wahrt, Carola Paepke (ed.), Potsdam 1993
(Catalogue of the exhibition in the Neues
Palais Potsdam, 11 September – 7 Novem-
ber 1993)

Exhib. cat. Turning Points 2004
Anna Werkmeister. Turning points/2004/
video/prints, Weimar 2004 (Catalogue of
the exhibition in the Galerie im Kunsthaus
Erfurt 2004)

Exhib. cat. Vedute di Roma 2007
Giovanni Battista Piranesi – Ansichten von Rom aus dem Berliner Kupferstichkabinett, Hein-Th. Schulze-Altcappenberg (ed.), Munich 2007 (Catalogue of the exhibition in the Kupferstichkabinett, SMB PK, 3 June – 11 November 2007)

SELECTED LITERATURE

Beaucamp 2010
Beaucamp, Eduard: Bernhard Heisig und die Folter der Erinnerung, in: Küttner 2010, pp. 10–15

Becker 2005
Becker, Marcus: Sammlung und Capriccio. Der friderizianische Alte Markt in Potsdam, in: Wehinger 2005, pp. 211–224

Beckert 2008
Beckert, Lutz: Jüdische "Entrepreneurs". Potsdamer Manufakturen im 18. Jahrhundert, in: Diekmann 2008, pp. 422–449

Bellamintes repr. 2001
Bellamintes: Das Izt-bluehende Potsdam. Reprint of the Potsdam original edition of 1727, with an introduction and commentary by Heinz-Dieter Heimann, Potsdam 2001

Berg 2005
Berg, Claudia: 33 Radierungen, foreword by Helmut Brade, Halle an der Saale 2005

Bergemann 2010
Bergemann, Uta-Christiane: Getrennt oder gemeinsam? Zur Arbeitsweise der Werkstätten von Johann Friedrich und Heinrich Wilhelm Spindler, in: Michaelsen 2010, pp. 192–210

Bettagno 1983
Bettagno, Alessandro (ed.): Piranesi tra Venezia e l'Europa, Kongreßakten (Venice 1978), Florence 1983

Bisky 2011
Bisky, Jens: Unser König. Friedrich der Große und seine Zeit – ein Lesebuch, Berlin 2011

Bleibaum 1933
Bleibaum, Friedrich: Johann August Nahl, der Künstler Friedrichs des Großen und der Landgrafen von Hessen-Kassel, Baden bei Wien/Leipzig 1933

Bloch/Grzimek 1994
Bloch, Peter/Grzimek, Waldemar: Die Berliner Bildhauerschule im neunzehnten Jahrhundert. Das klassische Berlin, Berlin 1994

Börsch-Supan 1986
Börsch-Supan, Helmut: Die Bildnisse des Königs, in: Exhib. cat. Friedrich der Große 1986a, XII-XXI.

Büsching 2006
Büsching, Anton Friedrich: Berlin, Potsdam, Brandenburg 1775. Beschreibung einer Reise nach Reckahn, Gerd-H. Zuchold (ed.), reprinted Berlin 2006

Christoffel 1997
Christoffel, Udo: Matthias Koeppel. Neue Bilder 1987–1997. Kunstamt Wilmersdorf, Berlin 1997

De Catt 1940
De Catt, Heinrich Alexander: Friedrich der Große. Gespräche mit Catt, ed. and translated by Willy Schüßler, Leipzig 1940

De Catt repr. 1954
Unterhaltungen mit Friedrich dem Großen. Die Tagebücher Henri de Catts 1758–1760. With an introduction by Helmut Greiner, Wiesbaden 1954

Diekmann 2008
Dieckmann, Irene A. (ed.): Jüdisches Brandenburg. Geschichte und Gegenwart, Berlin 2008

Diekmann/Simon 2001
Diekmann, Irene / Simon, Hermann (Eds.): Juden in Brandenburg-Preußen. Beiträge zu ihrer Geschichte im 17. und 18. Jahrhundert, Berlin 2001

Drescher/Kroll 1981
Drescher, Horst/Kroll, Renate: Potsdam. Ansichten aus drei Jahrhunderten. Bestandskatalog des Kupferstichkabinetts und der Sammlung der Zeichnungen der Staatlichen Museen zu Berlin – Hauptstadt der DDR, Weimar 1981

Eckhardt/Giersberg/Bartoschek 1996
Eckhardt, Götz/Giersberg, Hans-Joachim/Bartoschek, Gerd: Schloß Sanssouci, official guidebook, Potsdam 1996

Endres 1998
Endres, Rudolf: Preußens Weg nach Bayreuth, in: Exhib. cat. Paradies des Rokoko 1998, pp. 15–19

Evers 2012
Evers, Susanne: Berliner Seidengewebe in den Schlössern Friedrichs II., in: Exhib. cat. Friederisiko 2012, Die Essays, pp. 193–209

Evers/Zitzmann, currently being printed
Evers, Susanne/Zitzmann, Christa: Bestandskatalog Seiden des 18. Jahrhunderts in den preußischen Schlössern, currently being printed

Felgendreher 2011
Felgendreher, Daniel: Potsdam. Knobelsdorff ist nicht zu (s)toppen, in: Arch+. Zeitschrift für Architektur und Städtebau 46, no. 204, 2011, pp. 86–91.

Fick 2000
Fick, Astrid: Potsdam, Berlin, Bayreuth. Carl Philipp Christian von Gontard (1731–1791) und seine bürgerlichen Wohnhäuser, Immediatbauten und Stadtpalais, Petersberg 2000

Fuchs/Heiland 1925
Fuchs, Eduard/Heiland, Paul: Die deutsche Fayence-Kultur. 150 der schönsten deutschen Fayencen, Munich 1925

Giersberg 1982
Giersberg, Hans-Joachim: Potsdamer Veduten. Stadt- und Landschaftsansichten vom 17. bis 20. Jahrhundert, Potsdam 1982

Giersberg 1986
Giersberg, Hans-Joachim: Friedrich als Bauherr. Studien zur Architektur des 18. Jahrhunderts in Berlin und Potsdam, Berlin 1986 (unrevised repr. 2001)

Götzmann 2009
Götzmann, Jutta: Fritz Rumpf (1856–1927). Kunstmaler, Sammler und Museumsgründer, in: exh. cat. Sammeln 2009, pp. 46-56

Gottemeier 2007
Gottemeier, Rainer, in: Exhib. cat. Nordskulptur:licht 2007, pp. 28–29

Gottemeier 2010
Gottemeier, Rainer, in: Lichtparcours Braunschweig 2010, Stadt Braunschweig, Fachbereich Kultur (ed.), Braunschweig 2010, pp. 12–13

Graf 2011
Graf, Henriette: Die friderizianischen Schildpattmöbel, in: Friedrich der Große: Politik und Kulturtransfer im europäischen Kontext, Beiträge des vierten Colloquiums in der Reihe "Friedrich300" vom 24./25. September 2010 (URL: http://www.perspectivia.net/content/publikationen/friedrich300-colloquien/friedrich-kulturtransfer/graf_schildpattmoebel)

Heisig 2005
Heisig, Bernhard: Ruhig mal die Zähne zeigen. Über Kunst, Künstler und Gesellschaft, Peter Engel, Rüdiger Küttner and Dieter Brusberg (eds.), Berlin 2005

Heller 1987a
Heller, Gisela: Potsdamer Geschichten, Berlin 1987

Heller 1987b
Heller, Gisela: Der Alte Markt, in: Heller 1987a, pp. 35–58

Herzfeld 1993
Herzfeld, Erika: Der Schutzjude Isaac Levin Joël – ein hervorragender Manufakturunternehmer im Potsdam des 18. Jahrhunderts, in: Kaelter repr. 1993, pp. 177–226

Herzfeld 2001
Herzfeld, Erika: Der Schutzjude Isaac Levin Joël – ein hervorragender Manufakturunternehmer im Potsdam des 18. Jahrhunderts, in: Diekmann/Simon 2001, pp. 129–163

Hildebrand 1942
Hildebrandt, Arnold: Das Bildnis Friedrich des Großen. Zeitgenössische Darstellungen, Berlin 1942

Hintze 1930
Hintze, Erwin: Führer durch das Schloßmuseum in Breslau, Breslau 1930

Hoeftmann/Noack 1992
Hoeftmann, Inge/Waltraud Noack (eds.): Potsdam in alten und neuen Reisebeschreibungen, Düsseldorf 1992

Hofmann 1969
Hofmann, Hildegard: Handwerk und Manufaktur in Preußen 1769, Berlin 1969

Hüneke 1997/98
Hüneke, Saskia: Friedrich der Große in der Bildhauerkunst des 18. und 19. Jahrhunderts, in: Jahrbuch Stiftung Preußische Schlösser und Gärten Berlin-Brandenburg 2, 1997/98, pp. 59–86

Huth 1958
Huth, Hans: Friderizianische Möbel, Darmstadt 1958

Jacobs 1990
Jacobs, Renate: Das graphische Werk Bernhard Rodes (1725–1797), Münster 1990

Jacobsson 1773–1776
Jacobson, Johann Carl Gottfried: Schauplatz der Zeugmanufakturen in Deutschland, das ist: Beschreibung aller Leinen-, Wollen-, Baumwollen- und Seidenwirker-Arbeiten, vornemlich wie sie in den Königlich Preußischen und Churfürstlich-Brandenburgischen Landen verfertigt werden, 4 vols., Berlin 1773–1776

Kaelter repr. 1993
Kaelter, Robert: Geschichte der jüdischen Gemeinde zu Potsdam, 1903, repr. Berlin 1993

Kitschke 2008
Kitschke, Andreas: Der Potsdamer Palast Barberini, in: Mitteilungen der Studiengemeinschaft Sanssouci e.V. Verein für Kultur und Geschichte Potsdams 13/2, 2008, pp. 2–22

Klünner 1991
Klünner, Hans-Werner: Potsdam so wie es war, Düsseldorf 1991

Kohle 2001
Kohle, Hubertus: Adolph Menzels Friedrich-Bilder. Theorie und Praxis der Geschichtsmalerei im Berlin der 1850er Jahre, München/Berlin 2001

Kreisel/Himmelheber 1983
Kreisel, Heinrich/Himmelheber, Georg: Die Kunst des deutschen Möbels, vol. 2: Spätbarock und Rokoko, Munich 1983

Krückmann 2001
Krückmann, Peter O.: Das Bildnis der Markgräfin Wilhelmine heute. Ein Jahrzehnt Neuankäufe und Museumseröffnungen der Bayerischen Schlösserverwaltung, in: Archiv für Geschichte von Oberfranken 81, special edition 2001

Krüger 1779
Krüger, Andreas Ludwig: Abbildung der schönsten Gegenden und Gebäude sowohl in als ausserhalb Potsdams, 1779, Facsimile print, Hans-Joachim Giersberg (ed.), Potsdam 1979

Küttner 2010
Küttner, Rüdiger (ed.): Bernhard Heisig. Eine unendliche Geschichte, Leipzig 2010

Locker 2008

Locker, Tobias: Der Bildhauer Johann Melchior Kambly (1718–1782/4) und seine Prunkmöbel für die Potsdamer Schlösser Friedrichs des Großen, Typescript dissertation FU Berlin [2008]

Maaz 1994

Maaz, Bernhard: Johann Gottfried Schadow und die Kunst seiner Zeit, Cologne 1994

Manger 1789/90

Manger, Heinrich Ludwig: Baugeschichte von Potsdam, besonders unter der Regierung König Friedrichs II., 3 vols., Berlin/Stettin 1789/90

Markgraf 1894

Markgraf, Hermann: Friedrich Bogislaw von Tauentzien, in: ADB, Bd. 37, Leipzig 1894, pp. 443–447 (URL: http://www .deutsche-biographie.de/pnd117250686.html?anchor=adb)

Maruhn/Schmidt 2006

Maruhn, Jan/Schmidt, Carsten: Ideal Worlds in Potsdam – Potsdamer Idealwelten, in: Exhib. cat. Ideal City 2006, pp. 54–63

Mauter 1996

Mauter, Horst: Die Potsdamer Fayencemanufaktur 1737–1800, in: KERAMOS. Zeitschrift der Gesellschaft der Keramikfreunde e.V. 152, 1996, pp.79–102

Mauter 2008

Mauter, Horst: Masse, Glasur und Farbe nach Rezept, in: KERAMOS. Zeitschrift der Gesellschaft der Keramikfreunde e.V. 199, 2008, pp. 51–70

Mauter/Peibst 1993

Mauter, Horst/Peibst, Swantje: Barock-Fayencen. Kurmärkische Manufakturen. Entstehung, Höhepunkt und Niedergang eines Gewerbes, Leipzig 1993

Meier 2007

Meier, Brigitte: Jüdische Seidenunternehmer und die soziale Ordnung zur Zeit Friedrichs II. Moses Mendelssohn und Isaak Bernhard. Interaktion und Kommunikation als Basis einer erfolgreichen Unternehmensentwicklung, Berlin 2007

Michaelsen 2010

Michaelsen, Hans (ed.): Königliches Parkett in preußischen Schlössern, Petersberg 2010

Mielke 1972

Mielke, Friedrich: Das Bürgerhaus in Potsdam, 2 vols., Tübingen 1972

Mielke 1981

Mielke, Friedrich: Potsdamer Baukunst. Das Klassische Potsdam, Frankfurt am Main/Berlin/Vienna 1981 (2nd unrevised edition 1991)

Millenet 1776

Millenet, Peter Heinrich: Kritische Anmerkungen den Zustand der Baukunst betreffend, Berlin 1776

Müller 1977

Müller, Heiner: Leben Gundlings Friedrich von Preussen Lessings Schlaf Traum Schrei: ein Greulmärchen, Heiner Müller Werkbuch, Berlin 1977

Nicht 1973

Nicht, Jutta: Die Möbel im Neuen Palais, Potsdam 1973

Nicht 1980

Nicht, Jutta: Die Möbel im Neuen Palais, Potsdam 1980 (2nd enlarged edition)

Nicolai 1786

Friedrich Nicolai: Beschreibung der Königlichen Residenzstädte Berlin und Potsdam, aller daselbst befindlicher Merkwürdigkeiten, und der umliegenden Gegend, 3 vols., 3rd enlarged edition, Berlin 1786

Nicolai repr. 1993

Nicolai, Friedrich: Beschreibung der königlichen Residenzstadt Potsdam und der umliegenden Gegend, Leipzig 1993

Oesterreich 1773

Oesterreich, Matthias: Beschreibung aller Gemälde, Antiquitäten, und anderer kostbarer und merkwürdiger Sachen, so in den beyden Schlößern von Sans=Souci, wie auch in dem Schloße zu Potsdam und Charlottenburg enthalten sind, Berlin 1773

Oesterreich 1775

Oesterreich, Matthias: Beschreibung und Erklärung der Grupen, Statuen, ganzen und halben Brust-Stücke, Basreliefs, Urnen und Vasen von Marmor, Bronze und Bley, sowohl von antiker als moderner Arbeit, welche die Sammlung Sr. Majestät, des Königs von Preußen, ausmachen, Berlin 1775

Palladio 1581

Palladio, Andrea: I quattro libri dell'architettura, Venice 1581

Palladio repr. 1726

Palladio, Andrea: L'architecture de Palladio, divisee en quatre livres, translated from the Italian by Jacques Leoni, Pierre Gosse (ed.), Den Haag 1726

Palladio repr. 1993

Palladio, Andrea: Die vier Bücher zur Architektur. Nach der Ausgabe Venedig 1570 I quattro libri dell'architettura translated from the Italian by Andreas Beyer and Ulrich Schütte (eds.), Zurich/Munich 1993, vol. 2, pp. 197–198

Pleschinski 2011

Pleschinski, Hans: Voltaire – Friedrich der Große. Briefwechsel, translated by Hans Pleschinski (ed.), 2nd ed. Munich 2011

Richter 2005

Richter, Detlev: Stobwasser. Lackkunst aus Braunschweig und Berlin, vol. 1, Munich/Berlin/London/New York, 2005

Robinson 1983

Robinson, A.: Dating Early "Vedute di Roma", in: Bettagno 1983, pp. 11–33

Sangl 1991
Sangl, Sigrid: Spindler, in: Furniture History 27, 1991, pp. 22–66

Schendel 2008
Schendel, Adelheid: Studie zur Geschichte und Kunstgeschichte des Dorfes und des Schlosses Paretz, Potsdam 1980 (unrevised repr. 2008)

Schick 2008
Schick, Afra: Johann Friedrich und Heinrich Wilhelm Spindler, in: Friedrich300 – Colloquien, Friedrich der Große und der Hof, 2008 (URL: http://www.perspectivia.net/content/publikationen/friedrich300-colloquien/friedrich-hof/Schick_Spindler)

Schmoller/Hintze 1892
Schmoller, Gustav von/Hintze, Otto: Die Preußische Seidenindustrie und ihre Begründung durch Friedrich den Großen, 3 Bde., Berlin 1892 (Acta Borussica, repr. 1986/87)

Schneider 1862
Schneider, Louis: Das kurfürstliche Jagdschloss zu Glienicke, in: Mitteilungen des Vereins für die Geschichte Potsdams 1, 1862, pp. 1–30

Schöne 2009
Schöne, Katrin: Console Tables with Figurative Decoration From the Neues Palais in Potsdam, in: Furniture History 45, 2009, pp. 55–71

Schreyer 1932
Schreyer, Alexander: Die Möbelentwürfe Johann Michael Hoppenhaupts des Älteren und ihre Beziehungen zu den Rokokomöbeln Friedrichs des Großen, Strasbourg 1932

Seidel 1901
Seidel, Paul: Für Seine Majestät den deutschen Kaiser angefertigte Kunstmöbel und Bronzen auf der Pariser Weltausstellung 1900, Berlin/Leipzig 1901

Seidel 1910
Seidel, Paul: Bildliche Darstellungen Friedrichs des Großen im Tode, in: Hohenzollern-Jahrbuch 14, 1910, pp. 237–244

Sölter 2007
Sölter, Ulf: Die Vedute di Roma: Mehr als nur Architektur, in: Exhib. cat. Vedute di Roma 2007, pp. 16–23

Sperling 2010
Sperling, Jörg: Der Große König, in: Küttner 2010, pp. 42–51

Sprengels 1777
Sprengels, Peter Nathanael: Handwerke und Künste in Tabellen, continued by Otto Ludwig Hartwig, 15th collection. (section 1: Wallpaper factories), Berlin 1777, pp. 19–36

Staatliche Schlösser 1990
Potsdamer Veduten : Stadt- und Landschaftsansichten vom 17.–20. Jahrhundert, Generaldirektion der Staatlichen Schlösser und Gärten Potsdam-Sanssouci (ed.), revised by Hans-Joachim Giersberg and Adelheid Schendel, Potsdam 1990

Stengel 1958
Stengel, Walter: Alte Wohnkultur in Berlin und in der Mark, Berlin 1958

Stobwasser
http://www.werkverzeichnis-stobwasser.de

Straubel 1995
Straubel, Rolf: Kaufleute und Manufakturunternehmer. Eine empirische Untersuchung über die sozialen Träger von Handel und Großgewerbe in den mittleren preußischen Provinzen (1763–1815), in: Vierteljahresschrift für Sozial- und Wirtschaftsgeschichte, supplements 122, 1995, pp. 142–146

Thieme-Becker 1907ff.
Thieme, Ulrich/Becker, Felix (eds.): Allgemeines Lexikon der Bildenden Künstler von der Antike bis zur Gegenwart, Leipzig 1907 ff.

Thümmler 1998
Thümmler, Sabine: Die Geschichte der Tapete. Raumkunst aus Papier, Eurasburg 1998

Volk 1988
Volk, Waltraud: Historische Straßen und Plätze heute – Potsdam, Berlin 1988

Voltaire 1784
Geheime Nachrichten zu Voltaires Leben, von ihm selbst geschrieben, translated from the French, Berlin 1784

Weber-Kellermann 1990
Eine preußische Königstochter: Glanz und Elend am Hofe des Soldatenkönigs in den Memoiren der Markgräfin Wilhelmine von Bayreuth, Ingeborg Weber-Kellermann (ed.), Frankfurt am Main 1990.

Wehinger 2005
Wehinger, Brunhilde (ed.): Geist und Macht. Friedrich der Große im Kontext der europäischen Kulturgeschichte, Berlin 2005

Wendland 2002
Wendland, Christian: Georg Christian Unger. Baumeister Friedrichs des Großen in Potsdam und Berlin, Potsdam 2002

Zick 1992
Zick, Gisela: "Leben und sich freuen". Bildnisse und Kunst im Umkreis des Grafen Gotter, in: Jahrbuch der Coburger Landesstiftungen 37, 1992, pp. 91–126

List of Abbreviations

BLHA   Brandenburgisches Landeshauptarchiv, Potsdam
BSV   Bayerische Verwaltung der Staatlichen Schlösser, Gärten und Seen
DHM   Deutsches Historisches Museum, Berlin
GKM   Gesellschaft für Kommunikation und Marketing GmbH, Berlin
GStA PK   Geheimes Staatsarchiv Berlin, Preußischer Kulturbesitz
FU   Freie Universität Berlin
HAPM   Hausarchiv des Potsdam Museums, Potsdam
HH   Hessische Hausstiftung

HBPG   Haus der Brandenburg-Preußischen Geschichte
HU   Humboldt-Universität zu Berlin
LWL   Landschaftsverband Westfalen-Lippe
SBB PK   Staatsbibliothek zu Berlin, Preußischer Kulturbesitz
SMB PK   Staatliche Museen zu Berlin, Preußischer Kulturbesitz
SPSG   Stiftung Preußische Schlösser und Gärten Berlin-Brandenburg, Potsdam
SSMB   Stiftung Stadtmuseum Berlin
UB   Universitätsbibliothek

c.   circa (approximate date) / century
cat.   catalogue
cm.   centimetre(s)
esp.   especially
exhib. cat.   exhibition catalogue
fig.   figure
ill.   illustration
inv. no.   inventory number

l.   left
no.   number
p.   page
pp.   pages
r.   right
repr.   reprint
vol.   volume

Picture Credits

We have made every effort to identify copyright holders. If there are any omissions please contact the publisher.

Bayreuth, BSV, Neues Schloss: pp. 30, 43, 47
Berlin, Privatbesitz, p. 51 (bottom)
Berlin, GStA PK: p. 29
Berlin, Seidel und Sohn Kunsthandel: p. 51 (top)
Berlin, SMB PK, Kupferstichkabinett: pp. 11, 14, 36, 59
Berlin, SBB PK: p. 12
Eichenzell, HH, Archiv Schloss Fasanerie: pp. 23, 37 (2), 55
Potsdam, BLHA: pp. 45 (2), 46
Potsdam, Potsdam Museum: pp. 2, 24, 33, 34, 39, 40, 42, 48, 50, 53, 56 (2), 60 (2)
Potsdam, Anna Werkmeister: p. 62

Potsdam, Rainer Gottemeier: p. 63 (Simulation: Christopher Kühn)
Potsdam, SPSG: pp. 8/9 (photo: Wolfgang Pfauder), 17, 18 (photo: Michael Lüder), 19 (photo: Wolfgang Pfauder), 21 (photo: Michael Lüder), 25, 26, 31 (photo: Daniel Lindner), 32 (photo: Gerhard Murza), 38 (photo: Gerhard Murza), 41 (photo: Daniel Lindner), 48 (2) (photo: Wolfgang Pfauder), 54

© VG-Bild-Kunst, Bonn 2012 for the works by: Rainer Gottemeier, Bernhard Heisig, Matthias Koeppel and Anna Werkmeister.

Unless otherwise indicated, the copyright lies with the artists.

Plan of the Exhibition

Potsdam Museum – Forum für Kunst und Geschichte

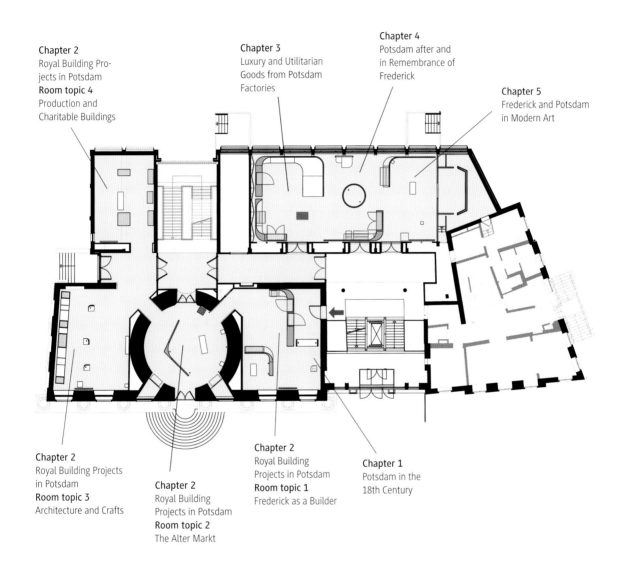

Chapter 2
Royal Building Projects in Potsdam
Room topic 4
Production and Charitable Buildings

Chapter 3
Luxury and Utilitarian Goods from Potsdam Factories

Chapter 4
Potsdam after and in Remembrance of Frederick

Chapter 5
Frederick and Potsdam in Modern Art

Chapter 2
Royal Building Projects in Potsdam
Room topic 3
Architecture and Crafts

Chapter 2
Royal Building Projects in Potsdam
Room topic 2
The Alter Markt

Chapter 2
Royal Building Projects in Potsdam
Room topic 1
Frederick as a Builder

Chapter 1
Potsdam in the 18th Century

Exhibition

Director and overall academic direction: Jutta Götzmann
Curators: Jutta Götzmann, Ines Elsner, Thomas Sander
Object database: Ines Elsner
Research for media stations: Ines Elsner, Tobias Büloff
Media station concept "Travel reports, Chronicles": Kathleen Grüner, HTWK Leipzig
Project coordination, conservational supervision: Oliver Max Wenske
Project organisation, loan coordination: Susanne Städler
Educational cooperation museum project: Jutta Götzmann, Julia Plato and Gisela Weiß with students of the HTWK Leipzig
Exhibition design: Duncan McCauley GmbH & Co. KG, Berlin
Exhibition architecture: Museumstechnik, Berlin
Posters and graphic design: Ecke Design, Potsdam / Berlin
Translations: English Express e. K., Berlin
Press and publicity: Elke Bahr
Tour coordination: Ute Meesmann

Catalogue

Edited by: Jutta Götzmann
Concept and co-ordination: Jutta Götzmann, Thomas Sander
Text editor: Thomas Sander
Editorial assistance: Mathias Deinert, Wenke Nitz
Image editors: Judith Granzow, Susanne Städler

Project co-ordination: Jutta Allekotte, Hirmer Publishing
Translation German – English: Josephine Cordero Sapien, Newton Abbot
Copy-editing: Michael Scuffil, Cologne
Proof-reading: Jane Michael, Munich
Graphic design and typesetting: Petra Ahke, Berlin
Cover design: Erill Fritz, Berlin
Production: Sabine Frohmader, Hirmer Publishing
Lithography: Reproline Mediateam Achter, Munich Unterföhring
Paper: Gardamatt Art 150 g/qm
Font: Generis
Printed and bound by Printer Trento, Trient

Printed in Italy

© 2012 Potsdam Museum – Forum für Kunst und Geschichte; Hirmer Verlag GmbH, Munich and the authors

Bibliographic information published by the Deutsche Nationalbibliothek. The Deutsche Nationalbibliothek lists this publication in the Deutsche Nationalbibliografie; detailed bibliographic data are available in the Internet at http://dnb.d-nb.de.

ISBN 978-3-7774-5841-0
www.hirmerpublishers.com

Cover: Studio of Antoine Pesne, *Frederick II of Prussia* (cat. 6)
Frontispiece: Bernhard Heisig, *Frederick the Great* (cat. 46)

With the generous support of

Kulturland Brandenburg 2012 wird gefördert durch das Ministerium für Wissenschaft, Forschung und Kultur sowie das Ministerium für Infrastruktur und Landwirtschaft des Landes Brandenburg. Mit freundlicher Unterstützung der brandenburgischen Sparkassen gemeinsam mit der Ostdeutschen Sparkassenstiftung.

von Rohdich'scher Legatenfonds – Stiftung des öffentlichen Rechts

Media partners